FOLLOW WE WILL

Stuart Thomson
&
Stan Gordon

Published by New Generation Publishing in 2021

Copyright © Stuart Thomson & Stan Gordon 2021

First Edition

The author asserts the moral right under the Copyright, Designs and Patents Act 1988 to be identified as the author of this work.

ISBN Paperback: 978-1-80031-211-1
ISBN eBook: 978-1-80031-210-4

All Rights reserved. No part of this publication may be reproduced, stored in a retrieval system or transmitted, in any form or by any means without the prior consent of the author, nor be otherwise circulated in any form of binding or cover other than that which it is published and without a similar condition being imposed on the subsequent purchaser.

We have received photographs from contributors in good faith, therefore the authors cannot accept any responsibility for copyright.

www.newgeneration-publishing.com

New Generation Publishing

Acknowledgements

To ALL our fantastic contributors for sharing their stories and photos from all over the world, to our proof readers; Fiona Desmond, Drew McBride, Barry McKinven, Steve Powell, Helen Baillie and Linsey Moffat. Claire Weatherley for the transcription and Lucy Weatherley for the great cover design.

To ex-players, John 'Bomber' Brown and Nacho Novo for their contributions.

Thanks to Tricia Gordon and all at the Stonefield Tavern. Thanks also to Hayley Copland for the never-ending support with IT and Jpg!

Thank you to Willie Vass, Photographer for the Andy Smillie photos.

Finally, to the long suffering HQ, (aka my wife Jo) for the Zoom set-ups (where is the link – Stan!), the hours of typing and reviewing, and not to mention all her support. Also not forgetting Ted (y Bear) the dug, for listening to the hours of transcript!

If there are any inaccuracies or typos, we apologise unreservedly.

Introduction – 1
by Stuart Thomson, Co-author

It is over a year since my mates, Drew, Ken and I, flew over to Braga for the away game in the Europa league and my last time in a proper football ground was, Bayer Leverkusen at Ibrox in March 2020. Little did we all know what was ahead of us for the last year...

During 'lockdown' people have tried their hand at all sorts of new things, from baking banana bread to learning Cantonese. I had a couple of ideas for my 2nd book, non-football related, but then I reverted to type. Stick, for the moment with football and the Rangers, my brain was telling me.

So, after a lengthy call to Stan, who manages the Rangers Legends and owns a Rangers pub, we agreed this was a joint project worth pursuing. Based on our Rangers contacts all over the world and knowing lots of Bears, who undoubtedly had a story or two to tell and share, here is the result.

We started the project early January 2021, and the response was phenomenal, from Scotland, Ulster, Europe, Canada, Oz and New Zealand, to name a few. My own travels abroad watching Rangers started in 1982, Borussia Dortmund away. It was like I had entered a whole new world. No longer was Aberdeen away or Chesterfield in the Anglo Scottish cup enough for me

From the pre-match pint in the pub, to the bus journey, which of course included the blocked toilet (if you were lucky to have a toilet!). Sometimes it was just a tube and funnel out the front door, by the driver, which must have been a delight for drivers on the M6, M1 or the motorways across Europe. There always seemed to be some dodgy porn videos on as well, once we were on our way. Changed days now with most people flying to European away games. Although I know some still travel by bus to far-off places.

I moved to live and work in London 1984, so it made trips to Germany, Portugal or Italy, that bit shorter, with me either getting picked up at my house in South London in the middle of the night, or at Dover for the ferry crossing

My brother Gordon ran the Shotts RSC early 80s, for a good few years and for a number of trips a certain Mr Jimmy Bell drove the Parks of Hamilton bus, if I remember correctly, to places like Boavista and Milan. I wonder what ever happened to Jimmy 😛

Over the years I've been fortunate enough to have travelled to about 70 European away games and one NARSA convention in Las Vegas in 2017. Some of my favourites were Marseille away 1991, we were due to leave a pub in Fulham about 8am, but after a big mix up there was no bus. Fortunately, T-shirt John, who shares a story later in the book, sourced one and we left the pub, very merry, 7 hours late

Monaco away was also one of the best, not just the score, but Nice just around the coast from Monaco is class, with great beaches and night life, albeit not cheap. We also sneaked into the VIP area at Monaco, got in the lift and who was there with David Murray and Sandy Jardine, but the one and only Sean Connery! As soon as we got out of lift, we were ushered away discretely!

On another trip with Jeff Holmes, the author of some excellent Rangers books, Jeff used to run a bus from Partick back in the day. We arrived in San Sebastian for an overnight stop before we left for Porto early in the morning. So we had probably been on a bus for maybe 18 hours, we hit a lively Spanish city late at night, what could possibly go wrong? Well at roughly 3am when we got back to our hotel, we of course hit the balcony for a wee sing song. In no time our hotel door was being battered, I opened the door to 2 Spanish police standing with rifles. It's amazing how quickly we sobered up. But it got worse, as we obviously fell into a drunken sleep, and by the time we were up, the bus was well on its way to Porto.

Still that train journey from San Sebastian to Porto was beautiful, especially as you come into Porto over that huge bridge.

Stan and I, despite being of a similar age, have only known each other for about 7 years. But in that time, we've organised a number of Legends games and events, from a Memorial game for Brighton Dave at Bognor Regis, a charity dinner for Fernando in London, the Ray Wilkins Memorial game at Sutton United, and only 2 years ago, a Memorial game for my big brother Gordon, at Shotts Bon Accord, after cancer took him incredibly quickly. Gordon would have loved contributing to this book and had many a story to tell, not all printable.

For ALL those who have contributed to the book, a huge thank you, I hope we've captured your unique story accurately. To 'Bomber', again a massive thanks for your input and encouragement. A credit to our great club. And finally, to those who have bought the book, thank you. We hope you enjoy the stories. If you are lucky enough to have been abroad to watch the Rangers, you know how good it is. If you haven't yet, I hope you get the opportunity.

Stuart Thomson

#FollowWeWill
@Rangers_Bognor

Introduction – 2

by Stan Gordon, Co-author

Co-writing this book with Stuart, was an easy decision. During lockdown we talk regularly about our team over the phone, from our different parts of the UK. Over the last 6 years or so, we have organised Rangers Legends games and fundraisers all over the UK.

The idea was a simple one, but it's been a phenomenal experience, Zoom calling fans all over the world. We chose just over 30 Rangers fans who travel abroad, to follow our club all over the world, we could easily have talked to 100, the response has been amazing.

For myself I have followed Rangers all my life. My trips abroad to watch Rangers, have been some of the most special moments of my life. I have been fortunate to have been in Europe with my father and son, so special family memories. From my first European game in Germany in 1983 where we lost 5- 0 to Cologne , to our last Euro adventures prior to lockdown. The game in Germany was the first time I had ever seen Rangers lose 5 goals. I helped run the bus from Blantyre, those were great trips, over on the ferry.

A special moment for me, was my first Euro game with my son Richard, and my Dad, three generations together going abroad to watch the famous Rangers, it was the best feeling ever. It was Bruges v Rangers in the first Champions League new format in 1993. I was President of the Terry Butcher Rangers supporters club, we left from the Union Jack club in Blantyre. As per normal we left by bus on the Monday for the Wednesday kick-off. We stayed in Ostend, after booking into the hotel, first call was of course the pub.

Some soldiers came into the bar from the German barracks, the Gerry Derry, and they were selling match tickets.

I managed to get to them first and bought 2 tickets for myself and my son Richard. Unknown to me, the tickets we got were for the Bruges end of the ground. Apart from 2 others on our bus Tam Thompson and Corrie, the rest of the bus managed to get in with the other travelling Bears. My son and I went into the home end. The Rangers end that night looked amazing and as usual for away games they were in good voice. After about 30 mins into the game, I decided I wanted to join in with them, so the flute came out and I started playing my heart out. Five minutes later there was a big circle formed round us by the home fans. The police then appeared with their truncheons and marched us round to the Rangers end, with me still playing away to the sound of the Rangers fans singing 'we are proud of you'.

We left the game with a 1-1 draw, Rangers played well, and I feel we should have won the match that night. My dad had boarded the bus to travel back to Ostend with all the rest of the boys. The police approached the bus and told my dad they must move on, my mates said to my dad, 'Archie you can't go and leave your son and grandson.' He said, 'Aye I can, he left me in Edinburgh at Hibs last week.' It cost me 60 euro for a taxi to Ostend, to catch up with the bus.

More recently I've been lucky to travel with the Rangers team on a few occasions. I treated my dad 2 years ago for the trip to Austria, v Rapid Vienna. I thought he would love it going on the same flight as the players and staying in the same hotel. When you travel with the team you must wear a suit, shirt, and tie. I can assure you it's not easy sitting on a plane suited and booted. My dad was nearly 80 at the time and he moaned all the way there.

The club had booked us into the Carlton Ritz hotel and after visiting a few bars we headed back to the hotel. I was drinking with my dad, Sammy Preston, Craig Douglas and big Harry Wylie, who owns the Bristol bar in Glasgow. I went up to the bar in the hotel and asked for a vodka, 2 whiskey, a gin and a beer. I had €20 in my hand to pay for the drink and the bar man said €128 sir, I nearly fell off the chair!

The morning of the game, the club ask you to get your stuff ready and around 11am you board a bus and they take you to a 5 star restaurant for lunch and then onto the game. I said to my dad and big Harry at breakfast, not to eat much as we would be eating lunch soon.

The restaurant was amazing, we were high up and could look all over Vienna, a stunning city. The lunch came, a massive dinner plate with the smallest steak you have ever seen, one small piece of potato and veg, you'd get bigger portions on a plane. We ended up sending for cheeseburgers from a takeaway across the road.

That night in Vienna was also one of the coldest nights I have ever watched a game in, but being with my dad was special, albeit expensive.

I hope everyone who buys our book enjoys it.

Stan Gordon

Foreword by John 'Bomber' Brown

James (Stan) Gordon and I have been friends for 47 years. We met, as 1st year students, at Blantyre High School. I played in the school football team, while Stan was one of our cheerleaders!

Stan aspired to be a footballer, but his inability to trap a bag of cement, put paid to that!! He focused his enthusiasm elsewhere, becoming the most loyal and passionate fan, his beloved Glasgow Rangers could wish for. He soon realised, he was able to combine his love of beer and football, to his great enjoyment

Stan and I have shared so many wonderful memories over the years, personal and sporting. When I played for Dundee FC, Stan would plead with us to beat Celtic, but for some reason, I always seemed to score against Rangers. On those occasions, I wouldn't hear from Stan for a few days after the game. When I got my move to Rangers, Stan was one of the first to call to congratulate me. He was delighted I'd signed for Rangers FC under Graeme Souness. Immediately after congratulating me, Stan asked in all seriousness... "Bomber, how you fixed for 30 tickets for every away game for the boys in the pub?"

The pub he referred to, was the Stonefield Tavern, known by the locals of Blantyre, as Teddy's. It's the most natural turn of events, that Stan is now the landlord of Teddy's. Made sense... he spent that much money in it over the years, he's bought it twice over! Teddy's is the only Rangers pub in Blantyre. Stan has done an incredible job, turning the interior into all things Glasgow Rangers – from the blue decor to the numerous items of memorabilia, celebrating our club's unequalled success

Stan isn't just a legend in Blantyre. His years of travelling the world with his team, celebrating with the universal

Rangers family, has made him lifelong friends the world over. Some of those friends, have shared their stories and experiences in this book.

Stan knows better than anyone, that Rangers Football Club has THE best fans, of any team, anywhere. They don't just support their team, they uphold the values of our great club.

I met Stuart and his family in London many years ago, he was organising a Fernando Ricksen night in the Union Jack club London, where him and Stan put on a great night,

A couple of years ago Stuart asked me if I would take part in his book 10 Matches, 10 Players, he interviewed me in the Stonefield Tavern, Blantyre. The 10 players attended the pub and told their stories, we also had a good laugh and catch up with the other ex-players, I once again would like to thank Stuart and Stan for asking me to do the foreword in the new book.

John 'Bomber' Brown

Contents

Acknowledgements	iii
Introduction – 1 by Stuart Thomson	1
Introduction – 2 by Stan Gordon	4
Foreword by John 'Bomber' Brown	7
Chapter 1: My Very First Flight	11
Chapter 2: Barcelona here we come!	16
Chapter 3: Over the water for my 1st Old Firm and what a Game!	21
Chapter 4: It's in the blood – the Rangers Family	26
Chapter 5: Thank you, Gaffer.	34
Chapter 6: Czeching in – A Trip to Prague	39
Chapter 7: A few wee trips with the Teddy Bears	44
Chapter 8: The Bochum Loyal	49
Chapter 9: The Party Bus To Athens	52
Dedication page to a true gentleman, Jim Baillie	55
Chapter 10: The Turin Shroud	60
Chapter 11: Dortmund via Amsterdam and a sore Face	64
Chapter 12: When John Greig tells you to keep the noise down, you listen!	70
Chapter 13: "I've had to block that Robert Duvall, he keeps phoning me"!	75
Chapter 14: The Baillie Loyal on Tour	79
Chapter 15: 'Haw Batman, whit ur you daein'	83
Chapter 16: Aki's Tours To Maribor	87

Chapter 17: Caledonia to Catalonia	90
Chapter 18: Flying the Flag in France	94
Chapter 19: Snowballing at the Acropolis in February	99
Chapter 20: 'Pass the ball Whittaker'	104
Chapter 21: 'The Ulsterman's match day'	108
Chapter 22: Groningen Loyal on Tour	113
Chapter 23: No Progrès for Pedro	116
Chapter 24: 'You're going where to watch Rangers'?	122
Chapter 25: Glasgow-Vienna-Benidorm-Glasgow	127
Chapter 26: Look who is staying in our Gaff!	131
Chapter 27: Some of our European Jaunts	135
Chapter 28: Vancouver to Peterhead without a match ticket!	141
Chapter 29: The Subbuteo Man	145
Chapter 30: The Union Bears' first invasion of Europe!	150
Chapter 31: Rangers & Romance	156
Chapter 32: We Best Keep Quiet, Then Bang, Roofe Scores	162
Chapter 33: We May Be Down Under, But We Still Follow, Follow	168
Chapter 34: A Final Wee Story	172

1: My Very First Flight

Bayern Munich 1 - Rangers 0 (After Extra Time)
European Cup Winners Cup
Final 31st May 1967

Story by: Andy McBride – Motherwell

Oh the good old days… A crowd of just over 70,000 watched my beloved Gers beat Slavia Sofia 1 - 0 in the second leg of the semi-final, to go through to the final on an aggregate score of 2-0. The final itself was to be held in Nuremberg, West Germany, as it was called then.

It was the stuff of pipe dreams to think of going there!

I was 19 years of age in 1967 and working in the Light-Section Mill in the nearby Dalziel Steelworks in Motherwell. It was two days after the Sofia game and my Da, Chick, a Train Driver, asked me, "Haw our Andy, dae you fancy going to Germany to see yir team in the final?" Now ma Da was never one for the football, so this came out of the blue, so to speak. "Who? Whit? Me? Are ye kidding?"

It turns out that ma Da was talking to a fellow driver in Glasgow Central Station, who was a member of the Polmadie Rangers Supporters Club. The club were looking for any number of fans to fill their quota on the hired plane. "Da ah don't think ah can afford it," I said. "Away and get yirsel a passport." was his reply. "I'll take care of things."

The next day I went to Motherwell Bureau or the Bru as we called it, along with my money and my wee photograph to get my cardboard British Visitors Passport. In those days I think it cost me 7/6 – (35p), a full passport was 1/10 (£1.50) or thereabouts. Anyway, I got it and I was over the moon!

Back then I remember going to Ibrox when we drew 2-2 with the other mob and going to a testimonial at Fir Park for big Charlie Aitken. I remember there were some good players on show including Davie McKay and Ian St John.

I was counting down the days until I was taking my first ever flight.

31 May 1967

I had to be up at 4.00am (never slept a wink, fiert I wouldn't wake up). My brother-in-law took me to Glasgow in time to get picked up and head for Prestwick Airport. I met up with everyone in Argyle Street, just up from the entrance to St Enoch's underground station.

"You Chick's laddie." a voice said to me. "Aye" "Well stand there the noo and I'll get ye fixed up wae somebody." A couple of moments later he introduced me to a guy who, if my memory serves me right, was called George Allison who came from Partick, and like me was taking his first flight. At 6.00am we left for Prestwick Airport; the journey had begun! At Prestwick, we were issued with our flight tickets and our match ticket with the cry of "Don't lose". As if!

I remember a giant Pan Am flight landed and a plane load of Americans must have wondered what was going on. "It's just crazy Scots," I heard one of them say. We had met up with the other clubs who made up the flight, the Rangers Song, The Sash, and the whole songbook was being sang. The noise was tremendous, no wonder the Yankee people said we were crazy!

In my excitement, my first flight passed by so quick I scarcely noticed. The flight took off on time, but I must add this wee story. Old timers out there will tell you in those days there was a procedure where on the plane you had to fill out a brown card with your name, address, occupation, and place of birth, plus date of birth. This was called the landing tax (nowadays this procedure is inclusive when paying for your holiday). Anyway, my friend sitting next to me was looking very downcast and when I spoke to him, he told me that he was down to his last ten bob. I said don't you worry, I spent the day with him, got him a few beers, as did his fellow fans. He was a good guy.

When we arrived at Nuremberg airport, the local TV station were in attendance. The male presenter was asking questions in German, the female presenter interpreting. When the last question was answered the female said, "off you go now, I'm sure you will find Nuremberg a very beautiful City." That's when one of the older guys with scarf and bunnet on, replied "Aye it fuckin shouldnae be, it wisnae that long ago, the RAF were bombing it." Red faces all around, the doll didn't know where to look!

It was a damp; drizzly day and we frequented the bars and shops getting looks from the locals. The Sash and Follow Follow were getting belted out.

This was also the time when the American GI's were stationed in Germany and they had never seen anything like us. "Gee man are you Scotties from the English Isles?" one of them was heard to say. "Do you know the Scottie racing driver Jim Clark?" to say we took the piss, would be an understatement!

On to another pub, where we heard the story about some of the Gers fans who headed to the team's training ground and showed some Gers players early editions of the morning papers. So, the Rangers players knew for a fact that the team were basically being slagged off as a team of half backs, not only by the foreign press, but by their own chairman, Mr John Lawrence.

Then on to the match. We were picked up at the pre-arranged large shopping mall. There were plenty of attractions there including clubs and bars. It was a well-known landmark and if anyone got lost, if they said the name, any local would know where it was.

The Game, no way did we deserve to lose.

My adopted friend and I were stood behind the goal end Rangers kicked into in the first half. I remember feeling this is going to be our night, we were giving as good as we were getting. There was just short of 70,000 fans in the ground, mostly theirs, but we could still hear the Sash and Follow Follow being sung loudly. Munich was only about 90 odd miles from Nuremberg, so it was really a home game for Bayern.

Gerd Muller, Sepp Maier and the soon to be named Kaiser Beckenbauer, names that would soon roll off the tongue, but we and our makeshift team gave them one helluva fright. My two biggest memories of the game were the goal that never was and the glaring miss by the same player, big Roger Hynd. No way am I blaming him, he ran his heart out, but no way was he a centre forward. In hindsight, Alec Willoughby was an out and out goal scorer, so why didn't he get picked?

Extra time was played and the inevitable happened, early into the second period they scored. A long ball into our box and Roth scored, I think he just got his foot to it before our defender. It was a sickener, their fans, who were deafening with noise all night, really erupted. I felt sick because the longer the game went on, I felt we had them. At the end you couldn't see the pitch for a ring of cops and stewards, but their fans made the pitch anyway.

We drowned our sorrows, (we were drowned anyway as the drizzle didn't give up all day) at a bar in the Mall. At around 3.30 am the bus came to pick us up.

When we landed back at Prestwick, I reflected on an enjoyable day I would never forget. I brought back many souvenirs which have fell by the wayside over the years. I still say we should have won!

But, five years later we did it in Barcelona. I just wish my best pal big Tam Kennedy was here to tell our story about that trip. Gone but never forgotten.

DIE MANNSCHAFTS-AUFSTELLUNG
Das Sportprogramm d. Südens
Welcome Rangers, Willkommen Bayern!
Hintere Reihe v. l.: Greig, D. Smith, McKinnon, Provan, Ritchie, Watson, Johansen, Wood, Millar.
Vordere Reihe v. l.: Manager S. Symon, Henderson, Willoughly, A. Smith, Forrest, McLean, Johnston, Wilson, Kinnaer.

2: Barcelona here we come!

Barcelona 24th May 1972
European Cup Winners Cup Final
Rangers 3 Moscow Dynamo 2

Story by : Archie Gordon – Blantyre

As a young boy I was brought up in Burnbank, in an area called the Jungle (no, not that one!) We had some famous people living there, for it being a small mining village, Big Jock Stein, the great Bobby Shearer, former Rangers captain and world champion boxer, Walter McGowan. In later years we had the late, great Davie Cooper and Jim Bett. Burnbank was always known as a staunch Rangers area and later the local gang would be known as the Jungle Derry.

I remember after Celtic won the European cup in 1967, Jock Stein was bringing the European cup back to his old school, Glenlee Primary, to show the pupils the cup Celtic had just won. When the local adults found out they took all their kids out of the school that day, so he turned up with the cup to empty classrooms!

There was also Jock's friend from Burnbank, Matt Wilson, who was Rangers daft. Matt was out walking up the back road between Blantyre and East Kilbride, the snow had started to fall and you could hardly see a step in front of you. A car pulled up next to him and the electric window in the car went down and a voice said 'Matt Wilson do you want dropped off at the house', Matt looked round and saw it was Jock Stein, he said 'f... off ya turncoat b......', he then watched as the car drove off in the heavy snow and he was thinking I have another 4 miles to walk in this snow!

This summed up Burnbank, a small mining village but staunch Rangers through and through.

I remember my first game, I was 12 years old and my uncle, Danny McDougall, was the bus convener on the local Rangers supporters' bus, Bothwell Haugh and Uddingston Rangers Supporters. The bus left Bellshill and picked most of the supporters up at Duffy's pub on Burnbank main street. We were playing Stirling Albion that day and if I remember right, I think that was the game Wullie Woodburn got banned for life. (sine die)

At that time, I was lucky to see so many great players – George Young, Sammy Cox and my all-time best, slim Jim Baxter. When I left school and I was old enough, I travelled on the supporter's bus to every game, home and away.

Barcelona 1972

I remember that season as being a stop start season, we did not begin the league campaign well and I think we went out of the league cup early, but for some reason our European cup run was better. Although it was the Cup Winners Cup and not the European Cup, all the papers at the time were saying all the best teams were in the Cup Winners Cup.

We drew the French side Rennes in the first round, followed by Sporting Lisbon, Torino and of course for the semifinal, the mighty Bayern Munich. The media were saying this should have been the final, the Bayern team were full of internationals and most of the team went on to lift the World Cup with West Germany. Rangers got battered in Munich but still managed to come away with a 1 - 1 draw. The second leg at Ibrox was as good a performance as I had seen from Rangers. A young Derek Johnstone being the standout player that night and two great goals from Sandy Jardine and Derek Parlane.

Barcelona Here We Come!

We were in the final for the second time in our history, this could be our time.

I went down to the travel agents and booked for me and my 5 mates – Alex White, Wallace White, Andy Findlay, Jim Dick and Kenny Weir. I booked us Tuesday until Friday, flights, hotel and match ticket – £44 each. A few days later the travel agent called to say they were sorry, but could we go on the Monday and return on the Saturday and they would give us some spending money as a thank you. I said, "Hmm give me some time to think about this." Thirty seconds later, "Okay then," I laughed! We stayed in Calella, a 30-minute bus ride to Barcelona.

The day of the match we took the bus to Barcelona and met up with the rest of the Bears in the centre. We could see early on that the Spanish police were not too happy we were there in such big numbers and it turned out to be the same at the game. At the stadium it was all Rangers fans. The reports were saying we had taken the biggest support to a European match, ever. There were no Russian fans in the stadium. I sat down in my seat and a voice said, "That's my seat you are sitting on mate." I turned round and it was a mate from work, we just laughed, I'll never forget it.

What a way to start a European final, we go 3 up with goals from Colin Stein and Wullie Johnston 2, as the song goes. Dynamo Moscow then brought 2 subs on in the second half and with not long remaining in the game they made it 3 - 2. The nerves then started kicking in but we held out for the most famous victory for our club. I think there was about 2 minutes remaining and the ref blew for a free kick and the fans thought it was the final whistle and tried to invade the park This was when the Spanish police reacted badly, one Spanish policeman pulled his gun out and I think if he had fired it that night, things would have been 100 times worse. John Greig and coach Stan Anderson came out that night to try and calm things down.

We boarded the bus back to Calella and the driver said "Sorry no Rangers fans on the bus." However, after I offered him 400 fags we were on our way to Calella! In the hotel that night, a Rangers' fan fell from the hotel balcony, the police arrived with guns and batons and told us to go to our rooms and stay there. On the Saturday, we boarded the flight back to Glasgow, the flight once again was full of Rangers fans and the drink once again was flowing, as we celebrated. When we got near Glasgow the Captain came over the tannoy, "Hello this is your captain speaking, Captain Kirk," I thought this is a wind-up. He said they had lost the landing papers and could not land in Glasgow until they found them. We circled Glasgow three times and by this time Captain Kirk was panicking. Ladies and gentlemen, we are running short on fuel, we need to find these papers, the stewardess then looks in her pocket and the landing papers were there, she had given the papers to one of the fans to write his phone number down! Typical of our supporters!

Since Barcelona, I have been on a few trips abroad watching the Rangers but winning our first European final in Barcelona was extra special.

I still follow Rangers, but it's mostly home games now, my seat is in the Thornton Suite. I am now good friends with Wullie Johnston and Colin Stein and speak to them at every home game. One game last year, a guy in the Thornton Suite asked me 'why does Wullie Johnston and Colin Stein always sit and talk to you Archie', I said 'because nobody else knows who they are, they are too young to remember them', so the guy had a good giggle.

I hope you all enjoy my story, and the book is a big success, I would like to thank my son Stan and his friend Stuart, for asking me to tell my story, it's been a pleasure.

UNION DES ASSOCIATIONS EUROPÉENNES DE FOOTBALL
ESTADIO CLUB DE FUTBOL BARCELONA
Miércoles 24 de mayo de 1972 a las 20'30 horas
partido final de la copa
de vencedores de copa
RANGERS F.C. DE GLASGOW
CONTRA
DINAMO MOSCOW

3: Over the water for my 1st Old Firm and what a Game!

Celtic 1 - Rangers 2
23rd August 1980, SPL

Story by: Warren Miller,
Sandy Row Rangers Supporters Club, Belfast

I suppose it all really starts for me with our annual family summer holidays. Every year was the same – the boot of the car packed with suitcases and bags, my mum and dad in the front and the five boys stuck in the back. It was straight to the ferry and over to Scotland and from there it was either my Aunt's house in York, England, for a few days, then off to the other Aunt's down near Bournemouth for a week or so. "Some miles I can tell you."

Or the other destination was Butlins holiday camp in Ayr, this was a much shorter distance from the ferry, as you can imagine.

Butlins is the place where it all really started for me, "My love for Rangers", I always knew I was a Rangers fan from a young age. Everyone where I came from in Northern Ireland were Rangers fans. Butlins trips were always tied in with a game, and my first experience was a sad one, unfortunately. That year my oldest brother Jackie got to go to the game, and I was left behind. I can remember the sadness I felt that day when they had left for the game. I said to my mum I was going to go swimming, but all I genuinely wanted to do was be on my own and feel sorry for myself. I ended up in what I can only imagine was a cinema type place. It was a bit darker inside, which was perfect for me. There I sat for God only knows how long, with my head down, in tears. Just then, this little old lady approached me and started patting my head,

"There, there," she said, then came the words 'his music would last forever' or something like that. That would all become clearer to me later. I was just about to tell her my sad story when out came a big brown purse from her handbag. One side had loads of copper coins and the other side had lots of silver coins. To my delight she reached for the silver ones and placed some in my eagerly awaiting hand. There I was outside, a big candy floss in one hand, Coca-Cola in the other and a box of popcorn under my arm, my sadness had gone. A couple of days before that 'certain singer' passed away, his name was Elvis Presley. I can only imagine that's what the little lady was referring to.

Just a few years later, my time was to come. It was August 1980, and we were back in Butlins, Ayr. I can remember two nights before the game, my dad nudging me and telling me I was going to see Rangers play the next day. That's when the excitement kicked in and it lasted for quite some time, about 48 hours to be exact. I remember waking on the Saturday morning feeling very tired, probably because I hadn't slept very much the night before, thinking about the game. Off we went to get breakfast in the large canteen at Butlins. My mum told me to make sure I had plenty, as it was a long day ahead. She also said I wouldn't be needing a coat today, that's when I looked up to the sky and it was a glorious blue. I knew then I was off to see a famous Rangers victory. There was me and my dad and four or five of his friends heading for the train up to Glasgow. It was a very warm August day indeed, which was unusual for Scotland, as it's normally cold! The train journey up seemed to take forever. I remember thinking we wouldn't make it, or we wouldn't make it on time, all sorts going through my head, but I looked around and everyone seemed happy, talking and joking, then the shouting started, the volume just went up and up "HULLO HULLO" that was the start of the singing and it lasted the whole day long. I didn't really know any of the songs, but by the end of the day, I knew them all, word for word. Off the train at Glasgow and then onto a large bus. I remember thinking, where did all these

Rangers fans come from? The bus was jam packed, I looked around to see if there was anyone my age, but it was mostly all adults. There was a young lad sitting opposite me, probably three or four years older than me. I was well pleased when he started chatting to me. I thought I had found a friend for the day. I think his name was David, he seemed knowledgeable about Rangers, obviously not his first game, unlike myself. It felt as though he was talking for ages, most of which I could not hear with all the shouting and singing. I can remember thinking, I really should contribute to the conversation, so I started telling him how it was my first game and how much I was looking forward to seeing Ibrox, his reply was as quick as his laughter, you won't be seeing Ibrox today, he said, we are playing Celtic away at the Piggery!

That was news to me! My dad must have forgot to tell me that small detail. I can remember feeling a bit embarrassed. Then out came his next question "where bouts you from mate?" "Butlins," I replied, thinking he meant where did I travel from. By the time he stopped laughing, the bus doors opened, and the fresh air came in. Thank God for that I thought, the heat on the bus would have melted you. One of the first sites I saw shortly after coming off the bus was police on horses, I thought to myself this is a bit funny. Where we lived, the police drove about in big grey Land Rovers, that we called meat wagons, it was only when I got closer to the horses, the fear kicked in. I couldn't believe the size of them, I wondered how the hell the police managed to get on them. Entering the ground was a bit of a squeeze, but once inside things opened a bit, well that was until the rest of the supporters got in. The atmosphere was truly amazing! Here I was, 11 years of age, surrounded by thousands of Rangers fans singing and shouting. In those days there was a lot more of the away fans allowed in, I think there were about 20,000 Rangers fans that day, in the old Rangers end. The first half got underway and the roar went up.

To be honest I don't really remember a lot about the game, a few chances at both ends and plenty of choice words shouted all around me. All I could think about was when we would score. It was 0-0 at halftime. The second half was much more exciting and we were attacking at the Rangers end of the ground, soon enough the first goal came, but unfortunately it was for Celtic. Tommy Burns had scored for them, the roar was unbelievable, I had never heard anything like it. Well not until the Rangers scored the equalizer. Davie Cooper came on as sub and made a great run towards the goal. He was fouled just outside the box and proceeded to take the free kick. It was saved, but then there was Jim Bett to knock it in. The roar was deafening, the ground beneath my feet was shaking, I thought my ears were about to explode and my whole body was trembling, I have never experienced anything like it.

1-1. I can remember someone close by shouting let's go for the winner. Soon after another roar from the Rangers supporters, but it was just wide. Then it came, the dreaded roar from the Celtic supporters my heart sank, I felt devastated. However, a few seconds later the roar went off from the Rangers fans, the goal had been disallowed, a clear offside according to all the fans around me. My excitement grew once again, then it came, a peach of a goal scored by Alex Miller for Rangers. Earthquake time! The whole ground shook, the noise was unbelievable, I must have been thrown in the air at least three times! Soon after that the final whistle went and we had won, 2-1 to Rangers! The journey 'home' to Butlins was great, everyone laughing and singing the whole way. By then I knew all the songs and I was singing my heart out, of course, always remembering to turn my back to my dad when the curse words came up. Everyone was patting me on the head and calling me the lucky mascot. One of my dad's friends kept calling me Wee Alex Miller, I was just about to tell him my name was not Alex Miller, it was Warren Miller, when he put his hand into his pocket and produced loads of coins, that was followed by everyone else giving me their loose change. Happy Days! I thought to myself. I could hardly walk off the train, I was so weighed down with coins. That was it, back to the holiday camp where the celebrations continued. I remember thinking I would sleep well that night, but every time I closed my eyes the songs were coming back into my head. One of the best days of my life for sure. I now belonged to the Rangers family and part of the best supporters in the world. I have been to many games since that day, but for different reasons the next Rangers v Celtic away game I got to, was some 30 odd years later, incidentally we also won that game, 3-1.

Some say I should go to every game at the Piggery!
W.A.T.P.

4: It's in the blood – the Rangers Family

Kilmarnock 1 - Rangers 5
15th May 2011, SPL

Story by: Gordon Watson – Auckland, New Zealand

This story starts somewhere near the halfway point in my love for Rangers FC, at least I hope so. But before we get to that, it's crucial to set the scene first. I was born in rural New Zealand in the 1970s, my father was Glaswegian, ex-Merchant Navy, British Navy Reserve and worked in the Clyde shipyards and trained as an electrician. My mother is from the far north of New Zealand's North Island and is of Maori heritage. Both my parents were raised in poverty, but with a fierce thirst for education and a love of all sport, but specifically football, which in our house, really meant Rangers or the Scotland national team.

My upbringing consisted of a lot of reading, a lot of stories about the old country and a lot of stories about Scottish football and the Rangers. We subscribed to various UK football magazines, took delivery of piles of Scottish newspapers, the occasional VHS cassette, watched football on the telly every Sunday with our lunch and talked about the game, local or abroad, endlessly.

This platform of Scottish football story telling consolidated into a remarkable happenstance in 1982 when New Zealand, miraculously, qualified for the FIFA World Cup in Spain and were drawn into Scotland's group. The build up to that tournament was unreal in our household – from being a wee bit of a curiosity, it suddenly became everything to all of us. We counted down the days to the tournament, to the opening game, Argentina v Belgium, then the opening game in Group Six – USSR v Brazil, and then our opening game – Scotland v New Zealand.

Scotland won that game 5-2 and I won't go into the details but suffice to say there was a lot of wind ups between my dad and I, resulting in raised tempers, tears and a red card for me, sent to school with the score at 3-2 and more than half an hour left to play.

There is a lot more to talk about here, but as this is a Rangers FC story, its best I get to the point – Rangers tour of Australia and New Zealand in 1984. I was now 11 years old and owned both a Rangers FC and Scotland replica tops (I even owned those shorts with the band through the middle and a pair of red umbro socks – full kit wanker). The Rangers FC top I had was the light blue pin stripe affair and I wore it every day, until it could no longer fit, at which point it went up on my bedroom wall along with all my posters.

We followed Rangers FC exclusively through the 1970s via newspapers from the old country and when video player technology came into homes, we would borrow a player and play the games on our old television. Dad would tell me stories about the Rangers FC teams of the 1920s and 1930s – he was a wonderful orator and his memory sharp, his turn of phrase colourful, old fashioned, but riveting. I put this down to the fact that in his day if you weren't at the game, you read about it in papers, or you listened to it on the radio or down the pub, or at work, so you had better have your facts straight, lest credibility be lost.

Scottish football made an appearance on New Zealand television rarely – World Cups weren't always a given, English football was staple and Scottish club football came in for the last ten minutes of an hour long show on 'Big League Soccer'. Dad talked about Jock 'Tiger' Shaw, Sandy Archibald, George Young, John Greig, Alex Morton and made them feel alive, as if they were playing somewhere down the road from us, they were accessible in my mind and pretty soon, they became fused into my heart and mind, the same way they had for Dad.

The Rangers FC tour of Australia and New Zealand was a long, drawn out affair. They were lined up to play Australia A, Australia B and New Zealand, due largely to the strong Scottish influence in both the Australian and New Zealand FAs. The best way to follow Rangers during May 1984 was to hope the New Zealand papers picked up the result overnight and published it the next day or catch news of a result over the radio - television news may catch footage, but it was touch and go and the time investment waiting for a piece lasting several seconds wasn't always rewarded.

Rangers were in the midst of a decline and Rangers may well have treated the journey 'down under' as something of a jolly. Some of the results certainly weren't jolly – two draws with Australia B, a win over New Zealand and a 3-2 defeat to Australia A. It's difficult to fathom quite what the Australian strategy was in terms of squad selection, but there was no doubt it was with the FIFA World Cup Mexico 1986 qualifiers uppermost in mind.

Rangers used the matches to play as many players as possible with some familiar names — a young Ally McCoist, Davie McPherson, Craig Paterson, John McClelland, Peter McCloy, Nicky Walker, the late Davie Cooper, the late Ian Redford, John MacDonald and Bobby Russell all getting regular pitch time with McCoist finishing top scorer on the Australian leg of the tour with four goals.

The game with New Zealand was scheduled for Mount Smart Stadium, Auckland, on June 11, 1984, a stadium more renowned for its rugby league and athletics, than football, although the New Zealand national team had made it their fortress during their 15-game qualifying campaign for the 1982 FIFA World Cup. It says a lot, that even today Mount Smart Stadium hasn't changed all that much – it has grass embankments, two tall, but old, stands and has not seen very much football in recent years.

The match was on television and after all the anticipation around it we never went. My father had an illness, brought about by hard living, typical of the men of his day, yet he worked relentlessly which would in the end catch up with him. Early optimism of tickets and a possible overnight trip to Auckland for the game waivered, faltered and then fell over, as it became obvious, we neither had the money nor a man in good health capable of leading us there.

On the day of the game, dad came to watch me play football and in the afternoon, we turned the television on and watched. We could hear some Rangers fans in the stands at Mount Smart singing songs I had heard many times among dad and his friends. The team that had qualified for the FIFA World Cup in 1982, was on the verge of breaking up and their stunning form from that campaign had all but evaporated – Steve Woodin and Grant Turner, two powerhouses of that side were on the wane, Steve Sumner, the heroic Kiwi skipper, had moved on.

Rangers lined up with McCloy in goals, McKinnon, Paterson, Dawson and McClelland at the back, Redford, McPherson, and Cooper in midfield with Clark, John McDonald and Ally McCoist in attack. It was a strange line-up and to this day I remember Davie Cooper, who I had come to regard as a left winger, playing most of the game through the middle where he gave New Zealand a sharp lesson in technique and passing. New Zealand were never in the game but unlike 1982 where I was all in with the country of my birth, there was no hiding the fact that this time I wanted Rangers to win, win well and so did dad.

We weren't disappointed – Dave McPherson scored the first just after the half hour mark, McDonald made it 2-0 before the break and Derek Ferguson made it three without reply on the hour mark. Dad downplayed the score line (I think because he saw Scotland choke on a three-goal cushion against New Zealand two years previously) but he couldn't get his smile of his face accompanied by a deep smirk of satisfaction that the colonials had been put away with a degree of swagger. I say this now with a smile on my face because a lot of that with dad was affectation, putting it on, you could say – he wasn't one to cut about the place putting others down, but by God, he did love Rangers winning.

My father passed away suddenly in 1986 of a massive heart attack and the day he died it became my duty to keep alive our relationship by continuing the love for all things Rangers. I had a modest playing career at semi-professional level in Australia, England and New Zealand, coached briefly, established a media and broadcast career in football and travelled the world to make a living from the game he taught me to love.

I've travelled back to Scotland frequently in the last decade and watched Rangers maybe 30 times in total and the most memorable of them all was Rugby Park, Kilmarnock, in 2010–2011. I landed at Heathrow the morning after Inverness Caledonian Thistle toppled Celtic 3-2 and the SPL title race had swung back in Rangers favour. I managed to get tickets for the Hearts and Dundee United games, both decent wins. We blew Hearts out of the water on a lovely, sunny day, at Ibrox - Jelavic, Lafferty, Davis on target with Hearts chipping in with an own goal. Three days later, back at Ibrox again, this time for Walter's last ever game in charge at Ibrox with Jelavic and Lafferty doing the business.

As a fan who was born and lives abroad, any game I attend feels special – I've missed most of the special moments local fans enjoy and perhaps, used to take for granted considering what was just around the corner for the club, so there was some pleasure and sadness in being able to see Walter do his lap of honour. This led into Kilmarnock and although I had two tickets pre-arranged for the Ibrox games, I didn't have anything lined up for Rugby Park.

As luck would have it, a former team-mate of mine, Steven Old, was playing for Kilmarnock and was in the squad for Killie that day and his good lady, sadly (or fortunately, from my point of view), had a touch of the flu, so Steve was only too happy to give me two season books. It was like winning the lottery, but I had no way of getting from digs in Glasgow to Rugby Park. Now, there's a lot of Rangers fans who bemoan the lack of friendly faces in the Scottish mainstream media, but due to my connections in the industry I'm aware of a few of them and friendly with others.

I decided this day to give the season book to a pal of mine, who shall remain nameless, but who was working at a red top, who was and is a mad bluenose. He negotiated some shift swaps, we grabbed his car and we were on our way to Rugby Park for what would turn out to be one of the greatest days of my life as a Rangers fan. The anxiety in the car was palpable all the way to Rugby Park but I had a feeling it was going to be our day.

Steven Old was a New Zealand international at the time and asked me along to watch Kilmarnock training a few days prior and the feeling I got from the session was there was a lot of players thinking about next season, getting a move, and without sounding uncharitable, and bearing in mind this was a one hour session, they didn't look entirely up for it. I wondered if that might be a sign of something to come.

Getting into Rugby Park was a squeeze, and the idea was to keep on the down low, find our seats, which turned out to be next to the families of the Kilmarnock players, and just try not to lose our shit if Rangers scored. We managed to do that for Lafferty's opening goal after a minute but by the time Steven Naismith and Lafferty again had made it three, we, and just about every other Rangers fan in our stand, had collectively lost the plot and were giving it everything.

Police Scotland had handed out flyers saying Rangers fans in the wrong end would be removed immediately but they would've been as well emailing it instead, for all the usefulness of it. I'm sure to this day there are countless examples of this, but my pal turned to me at 3-0 and said something along the lines of steady on, if Kilmarnock get one, and I just turned to him with a big smile and said give yourself the day off, we're champions elect!

Maybe it's part of my Antipodean culture to be laidback under certain types of pressure, but for me the rest of the match was surreal. Jelavic's free kick was glorious, I was sitting right behind the line of the ball and when Lafferty made it five it was all over. We stayed for the trophy presentation, took photos and videos on our phones, then drove back to Ibrox for the party.

We had to park some distance from Ibrox and as we were running toward the stadium, the team bus came up off the motorway with Walter Smith and David Weir sitting in the front with the SPL trophy, we couldn't have timed it any better. I waved like a complete idiot and Davie Weir waved back and as the bus pulled away towards Ibrox, everyone around us started to jog to the stadium, it was amazing. I loved every second of it and thought about Dad, how it felt like he was right there with me and we were jogging together.

I came back to Scotland through the Banter Years and had some fine memories and some pretty terrible ones as well. Now Covid-19 has left its mark on the modern world I, like so many others, can never be sure of when the next trip home will be, whether the virus stops us, or whether the cost of economy travel will be just too prohibitive to even make the attempt. Thankfully, we have a strong RSC here in New Zealand, the Kiwi True Blues RSC, part of the Oceania Rangers Supporters Association, of which, like so many others, am a proud paid up member.

SCOTLAND'S NEWSPAPER
Daily Record
CHAMPIONS 2010-2011
WALT A WAY TO GO
Smith bows out of Ibrox with his 21st trophy
32-PAGE HELICOPTER SUNDAY
£100k OF CASH PRIZES TO BE WON
FLEECED & FIRED
EXCLUSIVE Rogues Inc axe workers
KILMARNOCK FOOTBALL CLUB
2010 - 2011
TRIBUTE TO THE CHAMPS
3MENDOUS
Wonder Weir hails Three in a Row

TRUE BLUES

5: Thank you, Gaffer.

Rangers 2 v Everton 2 (Rangers win 8-7 on pens)
Dubai Champions Cup
8th December 1987

Story by: Gary Salmon aka Ging Belfast

I travelled to Glasgow from Belfast for a game at Ibrox against Dundee Utd December 1987. In the back of my mind, I had an idea to travel to Dubai for a Rangers game against Everton, for the Dubai Champions Cup. This being a game between the champions of Scotland and the champions of England, I did not have the money to travel but a friend from the Louden bar in Duke Street had previously said he would lend me the money, if required. After the game, I made my way to the Louden. I had a mate, big Fin, who was already booked up to travel to Dubai via Gatwick and Zurich. After a few drinks – I wanted to go.

My friend John Kedley approached the bar owner to borrow £500 and said he would replace it the next day. The bar owner also gave me a case of cider for the overnight bus journey to Gatwick. On arrival at Gatwick, I searched for a flight to Dubai. The only flight I could get was with Emirates at a cost of £470 out of my £500. The two teams flew out on this flight, free food and drinks on the same flight as the Rangers, I was buzzing and on my way to Dubai. After a few drinks I was mingling with the players in the galley at the back of the plane. I was sitting beside a guy from Sri Lanka who was travelling home via Dubai. The only Rangers guy he had heard of was Graeme Souness. Mr Souness, Walter Smith and Phil Boersma were all travelling business class, so I took the Sri Lankan guy up the plane to meet them. Business class was empty, so I just stayed there for the rest of the journey. On arrival at Dubai airport the two teams remained on the plane as the tv cameras were on the runway to welcome them. There was a welcome party held at the airport to welcome the two teams. When I approached the immigration kiosks, they were asking which hotel I was staying at. As I had no hotel booked, I doubled back to where the reception party was happening. Richard Gough then informed me the two teams were staying at the Intercontinental hotel which was just across from the airport. When I approached immigration again, I informed them I was staying at the Intercontinental hotel.

It was now 12 midnight in Dubai. As my mate was not arriving from Zurich until 2.30am, I made my way over to the team's hotel to have a look. When the teams had all checked into their rooms, I headed back to the airport to meet big Fin. When he arrived, we went back to the team's hotel and went straight up the marble staircase and started checking doors for an empty room. We touched lucky when an office door opened. There was a large table with green bias over it. We slept underneath the table. Next morning, we headed downstairs where Souness saw us and asked were we leaving already? We replied we could not afford it here, he sent us out to the pool and bought us a few beers. After a while he sent the Rangers team back into the hotel out of the sun. He came over to us with more beers and gave us the key to his bedroom. He warned us that it was bed only and not to abuse it. He doubled up with Walter Smith or Phil Boersma.

Ally McCoist had remained in Glasgow until the Monday as he had to pick up some award on the Sunday night. He was to share a room with Jimmy Nicholl. So, Jimmy Nicholl gave us McCoist's meal vouchers for the Monday. On the Tuesday morning the team were going training to the Al Nast club stadium. The gaffer took us training with them – we ended up hitting balls at Chris Woods. On the Wednesday before the teams travelled to the game, Jimmy Nicholl gave us 20 tickets to hand over to people he had met on the plane. He asked us to meet these people at the main entrance prior to kick off. With 15 minutes to kick off these people had not appeared, so the tickets went up in the air and were promptly sold. It got me a much needed few dirhams spending money; I informed my fellow countryman Jimmy Nicholl of this back at the hotel after the game.

Rangers were to go on and win the cup, beating Everton on penalties after being 2-0 down and having 6 goals disallowed by the referee. On the Friday morning I travelled over to the airport on the team coach helping wee Doddie with the team's kit bags on and off the coach.

On the way back to the hotel after the training session, big Fin lights up a cigarette on the team coach. Jimmy Nicholl cracked up. 'Who the fuck is smoking' he bawls out? There was a rule no one smoked on the team coach. Big Fin didn't know the team rules though.

Flight home to Belfast via Gatwick and the trip of a lifetime was over.

At the duty-free lounge on the way back, Trevor Francis was showing a young Ian Durrant which champagne to buy. I was in the queue behind Durrant at the cashier, he paid for his champagne and cigarettes with a £50 note and gave me the change, about £20. I was straight back into the duty free.

When I got over to Dubai, I had to ask my wee friend Agnes Fox over in Glasgow, who I stayed with when over for the game since I was 14, to call Harland and Wolff shipyard where I worked to say I had won a raffle prize to Dubai and I would need to take a week's unpaid leave. As I had no holidays left, it was well worth it!

A memorable trip with the best of people.

EVENING REFRESHMENTS

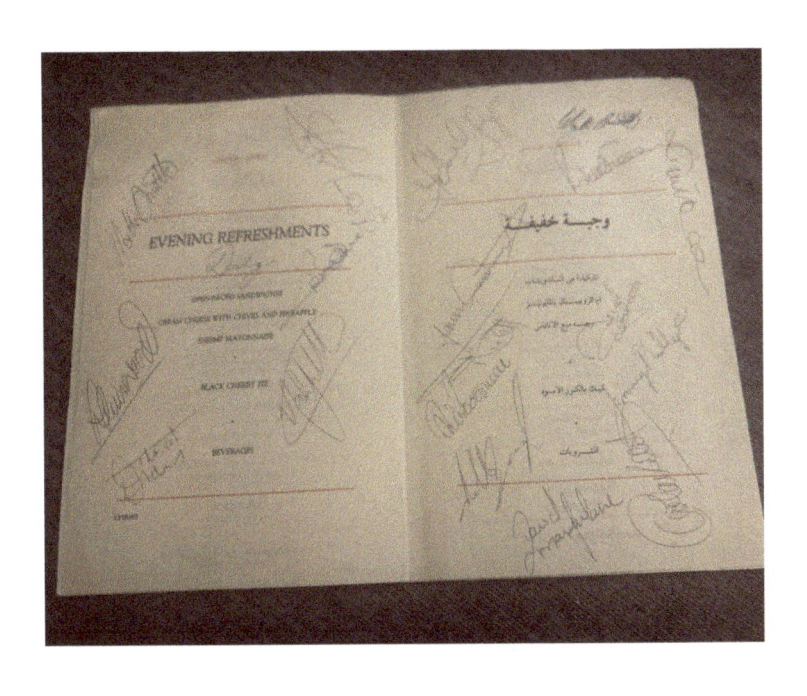

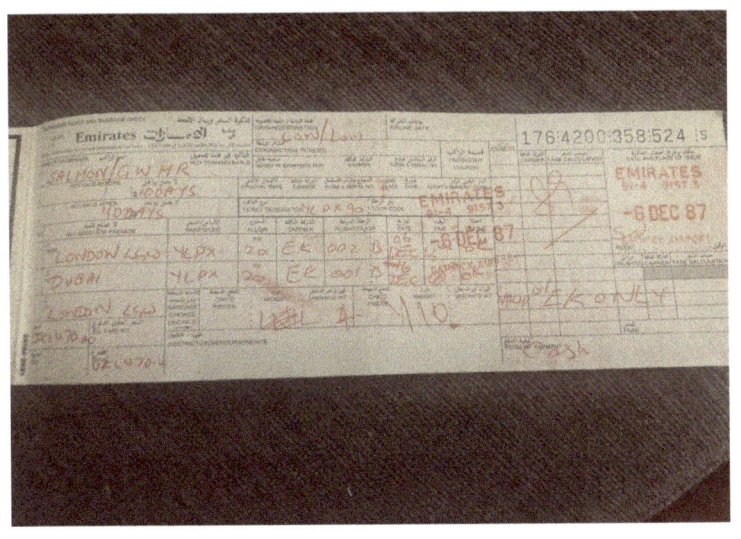

OPEN-FACED SANDWICHES
CREAM CHEESE WITH CHIVES AND PINEAPPLE
SHRIMP MAYONNAISE

BLACK CHERRY PIE

BEVERAGES

№ 2501
كأس البطولة لعام ١٩٨٧م
CHAMPIONS CUP 1987
EVERTON
Vs.
GLASGOW
RANGERS
افيرتون
ضد
جلاسكو رينجرز
AL MAKTOUM STADIUM
AL NASR CLUB
8th DECEMBER
ستاد آل مكتوم
نادي النصر
٨ ديسمبر
Dhs 30
٣٠ درهم
Emirates
كأس البطولة
لعام ١٩٨٧م
CHAMPIONS
CUP 1987
OFFICIAL HOTEL
THE DUBAI INTERNATIONAL HOTEL

6: Czeching in – A Trip to Prague

Sparta Prague 1 v Rangers 0
September 18th 1991, European Cup

Story by : John Mitchell, Toryglen True Blues Glasgow

Strange as it may seem to the new generation of Rangers fans who follow their team across Europe, 30 years ago and more, it wasn't just a case of clicking a few buttons online to book flights to anywhere in Europe. Before the advent of budget airlines and flights as regular as service buses, the only option open to most Rangers fans was to travel by bus, trips on which ranged from 12 hours there and back to Belgium, to 60 hours there and back to Bulgaria. So, when the draw for the 1991 European Cup (as it was still known) first round drew Rangers against Sparta Prague, the 30 hours there and back wasn't seen as too much of a hardship and the Toryglen True Blues bus quickly filled after being advertised by John Mitchell, who has been running the bus for nearly 40 years now.

The Linn o' Dee pub in Rutherglen Main Street, was the headquarters of the RSC three decades ago and it was filled with excited travellers from around 6pm on Sunday September 15th, 1991, as people began their trip in style and in preparation for the 11pm departure. The party was mainly made up of locals from the Rutherglen area and surrounding district, with people from Ayr and Motherwell making up the rest.

The overnight trip to Dover for the morning ferry passed noisily, although uneventfully and around 10 o'clock on the Monday morning, the bus pulled onto the ship and the travellers headed for a wash, breakfast, and the bars. Two travellers, having acquired bottles of perfume on the trip, saw it an alternative to the expensive lager on board and proceeded to drink some of it. The rest of the travellers, though, had made themselves comfortable in one of the bars on the ferry and had a surprise guest when Malcolm Rifkind, the transport secretary, approached them for a conversation about the game they were travelling to. When Rifkind asked them when they would be back, one of them said he needed to be back on the Friday, so he could sign on.

Arriving in Calais around 1pm local time, the bus made its way quickly to the German border and travelled on through Bavaria, stopping in a small town around 7pm, for an hour or so to get a break from the bus. Predictably, the closest pub was commandeered with big German stein glasses full of local brew being the order of the day. Moving on after a while, the bus arrived at the border between Germany and Czechoslovakia – as it was known then – around 11pm. Freedom of movement as we know it now was still years away, given Communism had collapsed in Eastern Europe only a couple of years previously, so armed border guards with savage dogs on chains introduced themselves to the party on the bus. Back then, people had an option of buying a one-year British passport if they were only going to somewhere like France or Germany for a short break, or a 10-year one if they needed to go on a more complicated trip. It turned out that the Czechoslovak authorities did not accept one-year passports, which was all a woman on the bus had with her. She was quickly bundled into the toilet on the bus and made to stay there while the guards searched the bus and checked everybody else's passport. The smell coming from the toilet probably kept them from searching it, so we can only imagine how the female who was hiding in it felt – remember the bus had been on the go for 24 hours and gallons and gallons of beer, wine and spirits had been taken –> for the duration of the search and for the length of time it took for permission for the bus to move to be granted. It's probably not an experience she would want to repeat!

A journey through the night brought the bus to Prague around 10am on the Tuesday morning and a drive around the city looking for a hotel to accommodate everybody, by chance, ended up at a place called the Hotel Luna, which took everybody in rooms of four, for £20 each. A couple of hours later and people went their various ways exploring the city. Prague was and is a magnificent city – and what was inescapable, was how cheap it was. The average price of the strong local beer was around 10p a bottle, vodka coming in at 60p a bottle. Rangers fans who went to Copenhagen for the Lyngby game the following year certainly noticed the difference.

Most people congregated in the bars around Wenceslas Square, taking advantage of the price of beer to sit outside bars in one of Europe's most spectacular cities. What was also strange to the Rangers support was the number of local businessmen who – as if it was the most natural thing in the world – spent their dinner break from work going into one of the many sex shows in the city for an hour. A bit different from nipping out for a sausage roll or a fag back home. The number of Rangers fans grew through the day as more and more buses arrived in the town to the extent Wenceslas Square at night resembled a Rangers supporters' convention. There were possibly 15 buses that had made the trip along with two charter flights so there were maybe 1,500 travelling fans in total, making as much noise as they could well into the small hours of the Wednesday, with the local off licences unable to believe the windfall that had presented itself to them.

Gradually the numbers began to drop as people faded and went back to their hotels – including one fan from Auchinleck in Ayrshire, who negotiated a price with an HGV driver to sleep in the truck trailer for the night – to sleep off the day's consumption for the game the next day. The same bars that had been filled to bursting on the Tuesday were busy again on the Wednesday before the game which – from memory – was an early evening kick off. People began arriving at the stadium around 2pm, Rangers fans taking advantage of the cheap beer to stock up for the journey home and for supplies for the few hours before kick- off. One off licence owner had an unusual security method – he had a huge machete to hand, presumably to persuade people he expected them to pay for anything they took from his store.

The buses were parked on a big grassy field outside the ground and must have resembled Glasgow Green on a summer's day as hundreds of Rangers fans sat down to enjoy the sunshine and the beer, before going into the ground. The game itself was a huge disappointment to a noisy and colourful travelling support. Rangers started brightly but lost to a fluke goal, a cross that caught the newly signed, Andy Goram off his guard and sailed straight into the goal. After 90 minutes it was time to contemplate the 30-hour return leg of the journey. Everybody was confident Rangers would overcome the deficit, plus there was a huge supply of Czech beer to make the journey home go a bit quicker. Lots of Rangers fans still had bundles of local currency which was worthless elsewhere – this was given to local kids who were hanging around the ground. It's unknown if they took it home to their parents or not.

About 24 hours after leaving Prague, the bus pulled into Swiss Cottage in London around 7pm, the idea being to stop until midnight and travel back to Glasgow though the night, arriving back when public transport was running. Everybody decanted off the bus into the closest pub with a regular complaint quickly being heard that London beer prices weren't the same as they were in Prague. Two queues formed in the bar – one to buy beer, one to use the public payphone as people called home to say when they would be back in Glasgow. The British are known for being mannerly, but one Londoner probably took this a bit far as he patiently waited his turn before making a 999 call for an ambulance to come to the aid of somebody who had been knocked down outside the pub!

Once the domestic calls had been made, something of a party took place in the pub with the Toryglen travellers and the locals who had been expecting a quiet Thursday evening pint. Come last orders and the pub closing at midnight, the bus set off up the road to Glasgow, arriving back around 8am on the Friday. The least said about the return leg the better!

7: A few wee trips with the Teddy Bears

Lyngby 0 v Rangers 1, 30th September 1992
1st Round 2nd leg

Story by: Andy Smillie – Glasgow

I could give you a million stories, from a million games. I drove all over Europe at that time to watch Rangers and what happened was, only way I could get to Lyngby (Copenhagen) was a one-way car hire from the UK to Harwich. Got the ferry from Harwich to Esbjerg, which was two days on the ferry, went from there for three hours on the train to Copenhagen. The only way I could get back was to come back with the Jimmy Clark Loyal bus and that was a story in itself. Which reminds me of another one, a match in 2000, away in Istanbul v Galatasaray where we lost 3-2. We went out for dinner the night before the game and we went to a fancy restaurant. In the restaurant there was a large party of people, including the referee and linesman who would be at our game v Galatasaray the next day. The referee happened to be Pierluigi Collina and as I was waiting for a taxi outside he came out. I had a load of Turkish lira and tried to give it to him and said make sure Rangers win. He looked at me with those big mad eyes and jumped in a taxi. I'm not sure I slept that night I kept waiting for a chap on the door.

Anyway, back to the Lyngby game, we won the game 1-0, wee Durranty scored the only goal late on, it was a beauty, what a player he was. Big Robbie Ferguson ran the Jimmy Clark Loyal bus, I had said keep us four seats on it for the way home. It was a double decker, that was parked near the ground and it was mobbed. I sat beside a Teddy, somebody had stolen a teddy bear and it was bigger than me, I kid you not. Honestly it was so funny.

We got a ferry back from Copenhagen and there was a bit of thieving… The Police were there with the big dogs. The boys had stolen the rolls and meat from the ferry restaurant and threw them to the dogs so they could go back in and do a bit more thieving. I know that shouldn't happen, but the fans on the whole were brilliant. Our fans at the European away games were and are, magnificent, second to none in my opinion. Then we got off the ferry, drove through Holland and down to Calais to get the ferry back to Dover and low and behold the boys were taking bits and pieces again out the duty free. At that time they put these wee metal detectors on the bottles, fags and perfumes. The security caught most of them and took them back, but as usual there was one idiot, who made a tit of himself. I was the only sober one, well me and the one who ran the bus, were the only sober ones. I don't drink and I said to the boys look, have you boys got any of the stuff because if we don't give it back, we are not going home. Then the Police came on and nicked one of the young guys. We went to the Police Station at Dover and they took this guy and said we need to verify his address and all that. I said look there are 70 on that bus, nobody is leaving here until the boy comes out. The big sergeant was alright, I said look let the boy out, we will pay the fine, whatever you want, the boy is just a daft young laddie. At this point the boys were all sitting outside the station, all singing, a guy on the bus showed his big bare arse to the sergeant. That made the sergeant's mind up and finally he said, "Get them all on the bus and get them out of here"… there is an idiot for every game, but it's all part of the fun.

There were probably more than 3,000 Rangers fans there that night in North Copenhagen, singing their hearts out as usual.

I flew to Barcelona in 1972, we went for £50, booked through a travel agent called McClure's in the east end of Glasgow, that included going to the game and two nights hotel. We were bussed down to Prestwick, off the bus onto the plane, it was an old propeller plane, I'm not sure it had an

MOT, but who cared back then. It got us there and got us back, but it terrified me and that was the first time that I had flown. I mean I used to drive everywhere watching Rangers all over Europe.

A pal of ours was married to a Dutch lassie from Rotterdam and we had arranged to play the local team in the 90s. It was madness going over on the bus and ferry and Ian Ferguson was with us, the Rangers player, he was not playing obviously, and neither of us were drinking. I could not go back on the bus, as I just could not face it, so I flew back with Fergie. That was the first time I had flown since Barcelona in 72, I still don't like it, but I fly all over the place now.

In 1967, I chucked my first job it because I was going to Nuremberg, for the final with Bayern Munich with one of my best pals, Jimmy Clark. We left Glasgow on a bus on the Sunday to get there for the game on Wednesday and then did not get back until the Saturday. We were really unlucky to lose that final to Bayern Munich. The game went to extra time, and there were about 10,000 Rangers fans and 70,000 of them. Years later, maybe about ten years ago, my daughter managed to get me the tape of the game which was in German; it was the DVD of the game; that was the start of the great Bayern Munich team. Big John Greig MBE was the best player on the park, he stood out like a sore thumb. Big Greig was always Captain Cutlass, do or die, a legend. By far the best player on the park.

I drove to Marseilles, that was a drive and a half, went to Bruges, drove everywhere and I think Bruges is the coldest that I have ever been. More recently when we played Osijek in Croatia in 2018, the team we bought Borna Barisic from, a few of us went out to dinner. We were in a restaurant that was right near the stadium, all sitting there, Stevie Campbell was there, and a few of the usual faces who go everywhere, but a few of them were steaming. Next, all the Croatian Ultra crackpots were coming up the road, all singing and someone who will remain nameless, was shouting out the window and the lassie working at the restaurant was terrified her restaurant was going to get wrecked. Fortunately, nothing happened.

Then another one with Pedro at Luxembourg. We stayed behind as we were going home with the players, everyone was arguing with each other, all raging and there was a guy there, I had never seen him in my life before, a big Rangers supporter and he was steaming. Pedro came to talk to him, and he smashed a bottle over his own head.

Then I remember, when we played Famagusta in Cyprus in 1995 and the bold Gascoigne was on the plane. I think he had a bottle of whisky and he was taking a swig out of it and one of the photographers took a photo of him holding it up to his mouth. This caused a big thing and Gazza was trying to get the camera. The photographer was out of order and we managed to take the camera off of him.

I'm probably one of the very few who has been to all the European finals; Fiorentina 1961, I was only young, but I wouldn't change any of it. Great memories and more to be made I'm sure under Mr Gerrard.

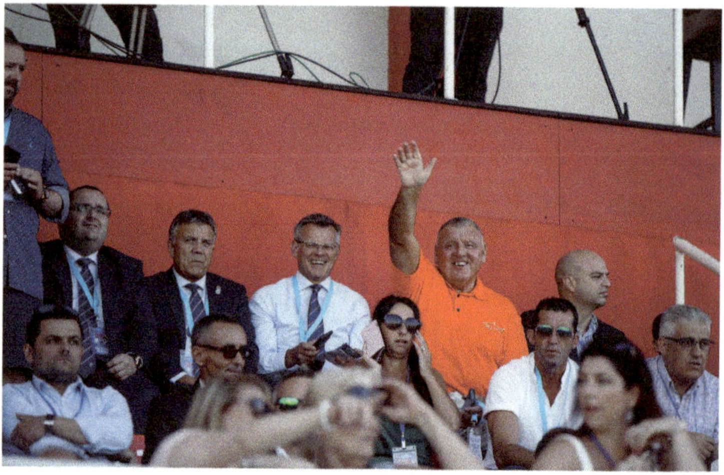

8: The Bochum Loyal

Friendships built from Rangers playing in Bochum v CSKA Moscow, 1992

Story by: Michael Ocker, Bochum Loyal RSC Germany

Since being very young we have always been interested in football from the island. It was therefore convenient that the great Glasgow Rangers would play their game against CSKA Moscow in Bochum, the place in Moscow was unplayable back then. Until today, nobody knows why the game took place in Bochum, it was hard to believe. It was clear that we would go to the game with some people. No sooner said than done, we went to the pub-Hopfendolde, at the train station in the morning, which was already very busy with Rangers fans. After some beers we got into a conversation with the Rangers boys and in the pub, it was getting fuller.

As we headed towards the stadium, Rangers songs were sung. The main meeting point was the fairground opposite the VfL Bochum club bar. Many fans came with buses that were parked there. Some Rangers fans also got lost at the Bochum Christmas market. When you arrived at the stadium you could only hear the Rangers fans, with their chants that we love so much. A few Moscow fans also got lost around the stadium. It was cold, but nobody bothered that evening, the guys from Scotland all ran around in T-shirts and jerseys, some gave them to us.

There were also many from the Rhine Army at the game, as they were stationed in Dortmund and the surrounding area at the time. The pubs around the stadium were well filled with the Rangers people, the atmosphere was good and there was a lot of singing and drinking. Then we went into the stadium, we watched the game in the standing area with some other

Germans. The atmosphere was bombastic for us. The Rangers won the game 1-0, through Ian Ferguson, which of course was good for the atmosphere. Some Rangers fans walked around after the game with large army hats from Moscow. Other Rangers fans bought trophies from the Bochum pubs and drank beer from them.

On that day we decided to start a German Rangers Fan Club, the Bochum Loyal RSC, and this is how the friendship with Glasgow arose, that we still maintain today. Years ago, now, but really deep friendships developed that have continued to this day. Since some Rangers fans have a friendship with Chelsea FC, we have of course also made good friends from London, we visit regularly and go to football or parties all over the UK. We also go to Europa League and the Champions League with Rangers and Chelsea, with our great friends to watch the team and the games that we love.

We will celebrate 55 in Germany, just like other Rangers fans all over the world.

Bochum Loyal R.S.C.
Stein 23'
Remember Barca 72
Johnston 40' 49'

BOCHUM
RFC
LOYAL

9: The Party Bus To Athens

AEK Athens 2 - Rangers 0, 10th August 1994
Champions League Qualifier 1st leg

Story by: Sie Leslie – GERS TV

It was the summer of '94 shortly after the World Cup Finals in the USA. European football commenced earlier than normal for the Rangers. We had Champions league qualifiers with the money-spinning prize of a place in the group stages for the winners.

Rangers had a pre-season friendly tournament to warm us up, the Ibrox International Challenge Trophy, featuring Rangers, Manchester Utd, Newcastle United, and Sampdoria. The Rangers finished in third place after beating Newcastle 1-0 on a Sunday afternoon. So it was a case of a few after match beers, wash yer baws, then off to the local bar in Tradeston, to catch the bus to Athens in Greece.

The Mount Florida True Blues ran the bus, but it had at least 20 non-members going, including my group. On this trip, two busses went together in a wee convoy, Mount Florida True Blues and the Kinning Park Loyal. It was myself, my brother Brian and Davie the Jakey, all aboard with our swally for the week.

As always, the bus rules read out, nae blagging and nae jobbies in the bus toilet, simple but effective. Some of the characters on the trip I remember meeting were big Finn, Robert from Newry, Matt from Wishaw, the Castlemilk crew Cammy – wee Rab and Neilly, the Peterhead lads Billy and co, Alex from Nottingham, All Bundy from Edinburgh, and wee Zippy from Drumchapel or Drumchurch as he insisted on calling it.

Two days on a warm smelly bus that had broken the nae jobby rule before the Kingston Bridge! We arrived at Dover, got the Ferry and off into mainland Europe, Italy bound for a first proper stop. Our bus arrived in Rimini on the Adriatic Coast for the day. The KP lads went to Ancona just around the coast. Legend has it one of the lads on the KP bus got accused of lifting shoes from a shop and ten guys from the bus got nicked; they were to be known as the Ancona 10. The story goes, that by the time big Stuart Daniels got back to Italy on a Thursday to pick the lads up on the way home, the cops weren't giving a damn about charges, all they wanted was the ten to GTF out of Ancona pronto!

There was no internet in those days, so the bus drops us all off, and it's every man for themself finding digs. 60-odd Bears hotel hunting, while drunk shouting "Baggio" to every Italian we saw. Didn't help right enough (he had just missed the penalty in World Cup Final) and had also been compared to a certain Stevie Fulton by Billy McNeil, so we were milking it big time. Finally, we got someone stupid enough to give us 3 rooms. At least no one was left on the street and we all did the double shuffle and squeezed in. Our room was stinking, smelly feet and swally, mixed with the warm sea air of Rimini.

Off to the pub for beers. Everyone met up and someone found a ball. Next thing you know we have a challenge match with the local beach guards. 11 v 11. Their 11 were made up of big strong Italian stallions, just think Amoruso and Porrini. Our lot, beer bellies, and fags. We had ten fit players and easily 30 pissed fans watching, so we needed one more and the Italians found us one of their pals that could actually play half decent. We pumped them, by means of a wee bit of cheating and kick fuckery (Brian and Zippy's skills) that meant they had to buy the drinks for us. Happy days.

At around 2am, everyone decides to crash out for a few hours as we had an 8am bus to catch. Everyone bar Davie the Jakey that is. Davie waits until we are all sleeping, comes up does a crap in the room bog and leaves it to stew in the Italian heat of Rimini. The wee night concierge thinks he has the easy night shift, but Davie decides to play a game with him. Every time he dosed off Davie buys another drink. 7am, wee Matt comes in the lounge and says, "fuck I thought I would be the first man down," and Davie says, "you are, I've not let that wee c*nt sleep all night."

Pay for a room and don't use it, that was Davies's party piece!

8am and onto the bus we go and when I say it was warm, it is hard to describe how warm it was, but on we went. The customary Bobby Parks tape on and away we go. At this stage we realise we have a problem, all the beers are roasting, so we have no swally. However, the Peterhead boys had a different idea, a stroke of genius in fact.

The new drink at the time MD 20 20 had just come out, and they had cases of it. If mixed with vodka and ice, it was the perfect breakfast for a long hot journey. The Rangers on tour, I will never forget watching the thick orange flavour MD pour out like jam and the ice and vodka making it drinkable again, a delicacy I tell ye. We're off on the next stage of our trip to Athens.

Just as we got near to Greece, a car with 4 AEK Athens supporters passed us making the signs that they would slash our throats. The full bus went wild giving it the old battle songs.

It was match day – YES.

So, ferry number two took us all around the Greek islands, with wee Zippy using baby oil to tan himself, while Cammy burnt like a lobster. Two blonde birds from Denmark happened to be on the ferry and went topless, so you can guess where all the Bears sat drinking. They needed a lift one said, to which the full bus replied: "Loads of fucking room yeah."

Arriving in Athens it was mental.

The cops took our bus to a local school type building and started to lock all the Bears in a cordoned off area. This wasn't like Glasgow cops, these fuckers had guns and they were angry men. It got too crammed and the Bears weren't happy.

We dedicate page 55 to a true gentleman,
who loved our great club. Now in Blue heaven.

Jim Baillie, 28th November 1954 – 2nd February 2021.
Gone but never forgotten.

In all honesty it felt very intimidating. Then out of the blue a gun fired above us. A cop with the gun shouts "I will say this once and once only, no more singing."

A wee Glesga guy replies, "Hullo Hullo" and its carnage, but the Bears are in fine voice!

Off to the match, they round us up in twos, with hundreds of police on each side hitting their shields to intimidate us. Up into a forest we go and at this point I'm shitting it thinking we're not getting out of here alive.

Eventually, they throw us into the ground 4 hours before kick –off; no shops open and no roof, but we we're there, that's all that mattered. Now we had to wait as more Bears came in, the guys that had flown in on the day, coming in at different times. They had a banner welcoming us it read 'Welcome to the fans and players of Rangers FC'. Lying bastards so they were, it was mental. The section to our left were the officials and player's wives and when the teams came out, even their wives were throwing rocks and coins over at us.

I remember asking one of the cops why the end behind the goals had a cage and he told me, "That's the mad boys' section, they hate the rest of the support, they will try and attack you guys later when you lose." I asked, what if we win. "You really don't want to my friend," he laughed.

The Rangers support was in fine voice as always, dodging the bricks, coins and rocks, while doing the dambusters. One of the AEK ultras managed to get a Rangers flag and burnt it on top of the fence in their section. To my astonishment the Rangers lad who owned the flag charged over climbed their fence and took the burning flag back – not all heroes wear capes as they say. AEK fans didn't react, I think they respected the fact the guy was clearly bonkers and kind of met their approval.

We had just signed Basil Boli and Brian Laudrup, but neither played, Boli I think was suspended. AEK scored once in the first half and again in the second half winning 2-0 with the Goalie playing out of his skin to keep the score down. I vividly remember the Nottingham Forest team who were out on pre-season, coming into the Rangers' end then realising how dodgy it was and leaving not long after kick off, Stuart Pearce, etc. The atmosphere was electric and their chant of 'Glasgow Rangers fuck off' accompanied by flying bricks and coins continuous.

It was crazy, but unforgettable. Just like pre match, we were kept in for an hour after the game, the traditional sing song, as always, kept us occupied while choking for a beer. As we left the ground we had the problem of finding our bus in the dark, while the cops were once again out with their batons. Some of their fans were still about; it was bedlam. I remember passing a bus full of them and one jumping out towards us. Big Garry Lynch shouted at him, then a cop wacked Garry with his baton (I can still remember the noise of it) it was pandemonium.

Finally, we got back on the bus and the long road back to Glasgow, with everyone safe and in good spirit. At this point we think that's all the carry-on over for the night, but how wrong we were. Due to being held back so late, we had to take an extra ferry to give us any chance of getting home in time for the Motherwell game, in two days' time.

A few busses filled with AEK fans, singing like fuck and banging the windows. They boarded first and it was clear they were thinking its only one busload of Rangers fans, but just then the KP loyal bus appeared behind us and came in together, now it was closer to equal numbers. Just before we got off the bus, we got warned any trouble at all, they will take the 2 buses in and hold us back. It's around 12 at night and on we get on the ferry, the Greeks thinking it's one Rangers bus. They surrounded the entry so we have to walk through hundreds of them. The two busloads of Bears got on and we all group together, I mind old Alex from Nottingham telling me not to worry, he will take two of them on! That made me laugh. The ferry departs, the bars open and a few of the Greeks walk over trying to suss the Bears our boys are all together as one growling pack. The Greeks started a chant to intimidate us and as it ended, there was a silence

The Bears were leaning over screaming it at them, not giving a fuck how many they had. The Greeks completely changed their attitude and appeared to bottle it a bit, they clapped the Bears and started shaking our hands. For the next 40 minutes, it was party time. It was our ferry now, but you could still feel the tension in the air, as both sets of fans re-boarded their busses in the darkness.

The long road home had begun. In Italy, we got local papers to read the reviews of all the flags in the Rangers end. The only one that made the papers wasn't even a flag, it was mad Cammy's T-shirt declaring "Castlemilk – it's on the way up." The bus arrived back in Glasgow around 6am on Saturday. A few Ulster lads and English boys on the bus stayed at my mum and dad's house so they could get a wee sleep, then back up we got and off to Ibrox to Follow Follow on…

Six days there and back, hardly slept and we got beat, would I do it again? Of course, I would, it was brilliant.

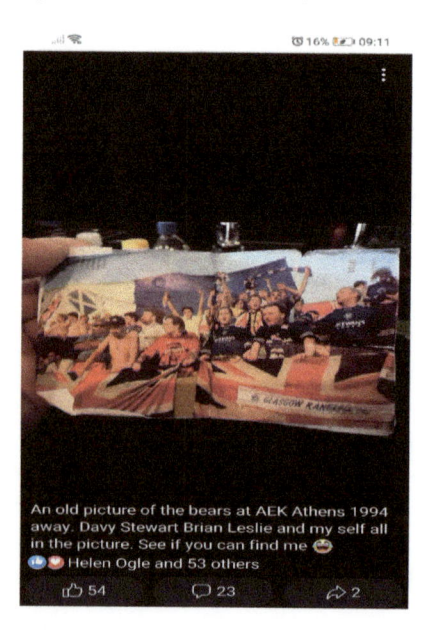

An old picture of the bears at AEK Athens 1994 away. Davy Stewart Brian Leslie and my self all in the picture. See if you can find me
Helen Ogle and 53 others

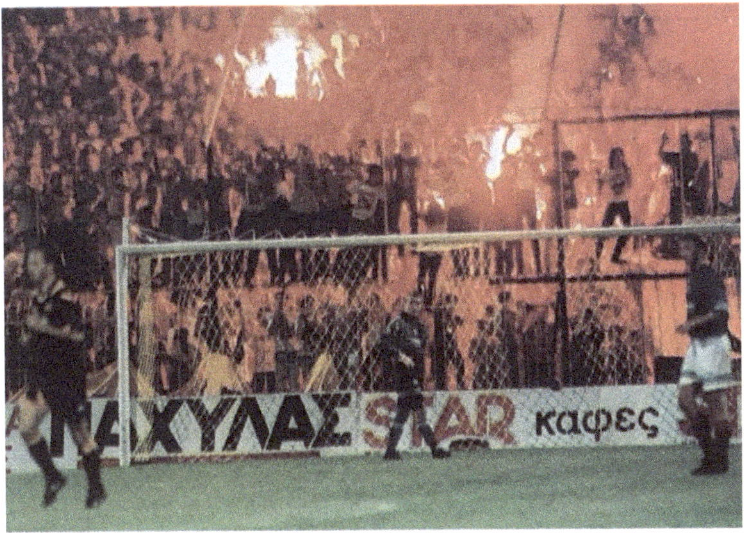
STAR
καφες

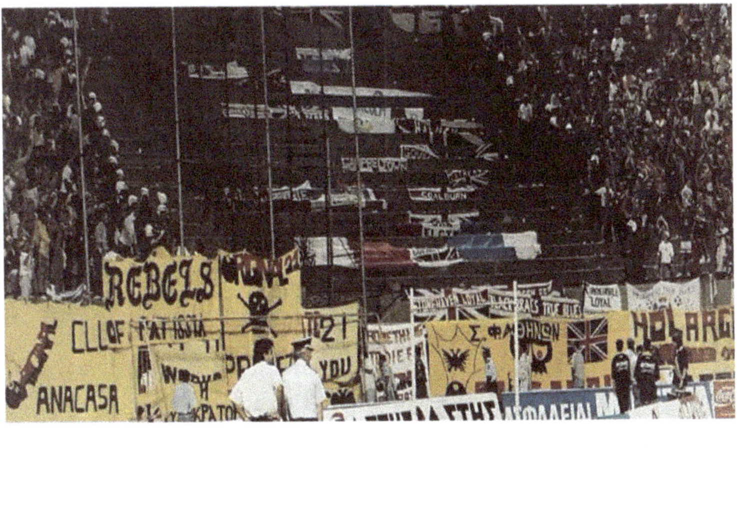
REBELS
ANACASA

10: The Turin Shroud

Juventus 4 - Rangers 1 – 18th October 1995
Champions League

Story by: John Slowey, Sussex England

We went with a crowd of my mates from London and other boys from all over the UK. I think it was Wullie and Stevie from East Kilbride, Chukka from Boro, Alex and Billy (who had a wee accident in his troosers). We chose to go with Flight Options; we had been with them a few times, some guys from Manchester ran Flight Options. Heathrow was our departure point and we all met up, having a good few beers on the plane and we were expecting to arrive in Turin in a couple of hours. Annoyingly there was terrible weather, so we were diverted to Milan. Before you knew it we were in Milan and the guys from Flight Options are trying to get a bus to get us up to Turin. We had a couple of beers at the airport, next thing they had managed to get a bus, so there were 50 of us on a bus going up to Turin to watch Rangers. However, the guys from Flight Options, in their infinite wisdom thought that there was no way we could bring any booze onto the bus, which was obviously a recipe for disaster. The Bears got on the bus, there is no booze, the troops were going mental, saying look we are out for a football game here, we need to get a couple of beers from somewhere. I went up to the 2 Manc guys and I said look, this is not going to work, they are all going off their heads here. I went up to speak to the driver and I said to all the boys on the bus, look let's have a whip round, give the driver a couple of quid each, may have even been lira back then, so he pulled into a service station and we managed to get all the beers and some wines for the journey up to Turin. The driver was chuffed to bits!

We arrived in Turin and we were having a few beers in a cracking wee bar, having a great time, a sing song, seeing people who flew over as usual; some other people from London, Surrey, people from back home in Scotland, it was brilliant. It was then time to head up towards the big Juventus stadium, singing away. Next minute, as we turned the corner (there were only about 12 of us maybe) there were about 50 Juventus fans coming towards us. We thought they were only coming to swap scarfs, but before we knew it, we were getting a right doing from them. They were pulling knives out, I got hit over the head by a bicycle chain; right down the side of my face. One of the boys got bottled. It was carnage. Some other people tried to stop it and then the Italian Police came in. A few of us were in a right mess, we got taken into the ground to the First Aid place and got patched up. A few of the Rangers officials came in to make sure we were ok, I think one of them was the wee bald guy, Alistair Hood. Out on the pitch Rangers were getting beat anyway, I think we were 3-0 down at this point by the time we even got out to see any of the game. We did see Ravanelli score their 4th goal, and big Goughie scored from a rare shot, with the help of a wee deflection. I think we were lucky to get away with 4-1, but I tell you what, the atmosphere inside that stadium was one of the best, despite what happened to us.

Things took another unfortunate turn when we went back to Turin airport. We were in the departure lounge and a few of the Bears had been misbehaving; maybe nicking a few things from Duty Free. We were due to get on the flight, but one of the Rangers boys had either been drunk on boarding or said something offensive to one of the Air Stewardesses and before we knew it, we were put into a holding bay; they were not letting us get on the flight and it took off without us, we were stuck in Turin airport. Nightmare in Turin.

We were hanging about the airport and I was trying to act as a peacemaker. The police had their batons and everything ready and we thought we were going to get smashed to bits, but I had a chat with this officer, who happened to be a Roma, but also a Rangers fan. I said to him, look what can we do here? He said just try and keep the noise down and we will see what we can do. He had a look at my jacket, I had one of those big winter coats on with the Rangers badge on it and he said, I like that, so I decided to try and negotiate a deal. I said listen if I give you this coat, how about trying to smooth things out and see if we can get sorted for a flight back. As a result, the police calmed down a bit, backed off and they left us to sleep in this holding bay and the next morning we were on a flight back to London. Everybody was as quiet as a mouse for obvious reasons; we just wanted to get back home. There were no mobile phones or anything, so you couldn't phone home. We were all queuing up, trying to get to the one phone to call our other halves / parents to say we were being held up here. That was Juventus away, not the happiest of trips on or off the pitch, but definitely memorable!

I was born and bred in Glasgow, near Shawfield Stadium, but I was really brought up in East Kilbride. I moved out to East Kilbride and then in the 80's spent a good twenty odd years' in London; that is where I met Stuart who is co-authoring the book and I've met Stan at Rangers Legends events and away trips over the years as well. For the last few years, I have been down in Sussex. I am a member of Surrey True Blues and I go to most European away games and get up to Ibrox as often as I can being a season ticket holder.

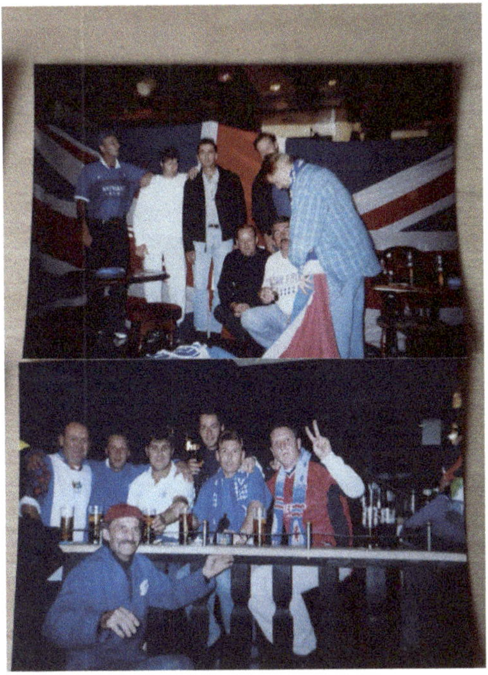

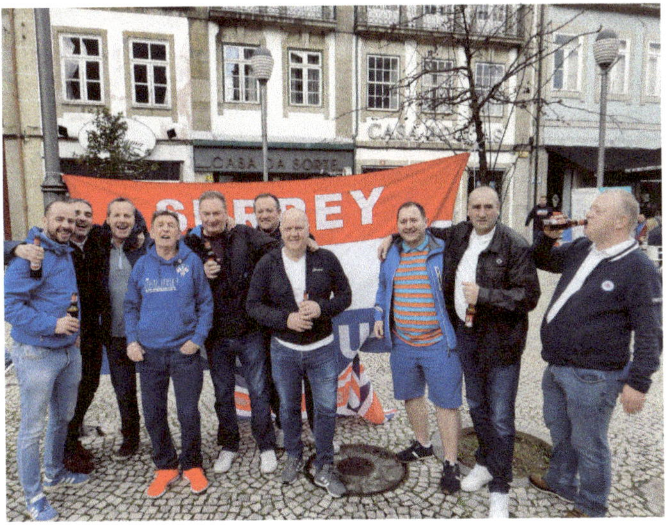
CASA DA SORTE

11: Dortmund via Amsterdam and a sore Face

Borussia Dortmund 2 - Rangers 2
5th Dec 1995, Champions League

Story by: Dougie Dick – Kent, England, Member of London RSC

Although born in Ayrshire, I grew up in Blairgowrie, Perthshire, fostered at 10 months by Ronald and Frances Dick. I had amazing parents, but I cannot pin my devotion to Rangers on them, as they were not hugely into any sport. Most people outside of Blairgowrie would not recognise the town as a hotbed of Rangers supporters. However, the huge number of raspberry fields in the area and the opportunities of work they provided, led to a significant number of Glaswegians settling there. So, growing up as a small boy, everyone who mattered, even during the other mobs nine in a row era, seemed to be a bear.

There was no bigger Rangers family than the Carmichaels, who lived around the corner in Craighall Place. Father Jimmy, sons Dirk and Rory and of course their friend John Derry Duncan, I looked up to them with awe and I hungered to follow, follow, as they did. Rory has become a friend and it has been great to bump into him in many foreign fields over the years. My headmaster at Blair High, the legend, Mr Alexander Dunlop was also a huge bear and his son Dave, and I used to travel to games during our school days, including hitching a lift from a nun once!

Working and living in Forfar in a retail shop, meant that on Saturday's I could hardly get to games. So, in 1986 I sold my car and moved to London to look for new work opportunities and track down the local supporter's club,

Rangers FCSA London Branch. Within a couple of years, I had my dream job working as a rep in the licensed trade, a job I love, and I am still doing today, for Britain's oldest Brewery. The experience of organising events and people would hold me in good stead for this story and many other Rangers trips I have organised.

By 1995 I was a seasoned campaigner traveling to watch Rangers both domestically and for European away games, and I was by now the ticket/travel secretary for the London Branch. Previously I had tended to make my own way to the away games in Europe or with my good friend and son's Godfather, Paul Langley and his supporter's club UK Loyal. However, the London Branch members wanted to travel to the last Champions league away fixture as an organised club trip by coach as the other two away ties that season were easier by air.

We contacted Rangers for tickets and to run our coach but initially we were turned down. We found out that Ging (Gary Salmon) and the East Belfast boys had a similar problem so we asked if we could share a bus with them. Rangers said yes, but only if we used their designated coach supplier, Parks of Hamilton, so we filled our share of the seats and looked ahead to what we thought would be an easy and trouble-free trip.

Well Monday the 4th December arrived, and the Parks bus had collected Ging and party at Stranraer and headed to meet us in London. The first problem was that before they left Belfast a few of the locals who had been incarcerated in the Troubles and recently been released, decided they would like to go as well. We found this out when they arrived to pick us up and there was a shortage of seats. Thankfully the two coach drivers did not object to the overload and as Ging explained to me, he wasn't going to ask those who hadn't booked to get off, so we had a short journey from London to Dover with three to a seat and some on the floor or standing.

At least we will get some relaxation on the ferry I foolishly thought. Sitting down with the lads having some drinks and over the tannoid system I hear, "Will Douglas Dick and Gary

Salmon please report to the office," wtf?! I find Ging and we head there, the Captain straight to the point, "Tell your party that if they do not return the stolen goods to the duty-free shop, you will all be deported back to Dover where you will be arrested." Thankfully, the guilty parties returned the goods and we managed to set off to Amsterdam. As usual on a supporter's coach, the drinks flowed, so did the banter and the cultural tunes were blaring and as tradition goes, the toilet was blocked.

On arrival in Amsterdam, we checked into our accommodation and out into the night we went in our various groups. To my memory we were the only supporter's bus in the city that night, which meant that some of the local hooligans must have known, but more of that later. As you do in Dam, most of the lads were in various pubs in the Red-Light District, I was with pals Jim Cowie, Jim's mate also Jim, Marcus Hopkins and Nevil Balcombe. Nevil unfortunately passed away a couple of years ago, a great lad and sorely missed. The evening initially was calm and uneventful, we had been in a few bars, tried some of the local culture bars including their unique cakes.

One of the lads wanted to do some window shopping, and while he was making up his mind, a massive group of guys came round the corner and we could tell they were not the friendly type. Remember, we had been drinking and enjoying cakes so were in no fit state to defend ourselves. A huge bloke launched a punch at me, connected and down I went, mind you he could have probably blown me over. While lying on the cobbles I heard two loud splashes, which I knew would be two of my friends who had been launched into a canal. I knew I was up next when the Dutch thugs went to pick me up. Then the police arrived and I was saved the embarrassment of joining my mates in the water, but instead I was dropped by the head onto the cobbles. The police took us all to the local station, in my confusion I thought we had been arrested, but they only wanted statements and check we were all okay and to give dry overalls to both Jim Cowie and Marcus.

The next morning with my face aching and head throbbing, I took my place on the overcrowded bus. I had arranged with Parks that we travel via Arnhem so we could visit and pay our respects at the Airborne War Cemetery. We headed there first, whilst I took the slagging of a lifetime from my old friend Frankie Shanks of Belfast fame. This banter on the coach was a perfect remedy to distract me from my pain. The stop off at Arnhem was very moving and the coach was quiet for short period afterwards.

On arrival in Dortmund, it seemed we had landed in the coldest place in the world, it was certainly the coldest I had been at a game, -14 so I believe. As my face was still throbbing, one of the guys I know offered me some powder to put on my lips which helped numb the pain and then the drink kicked in, which meant I forgot about it entirely. We headed off to the match much later, it was a dead rubber as we were already out, and Dortmund had qualified in second place. The Rangers end as usual was packed, noisy and despite the freezing cold weather, there were still some bears with short sleeves or no shirts at all. There had been some doubt regarding the game going ahead due to the weather, but it did and thankfully it was a good game. We took the lead through Laudrup, then fell 2-1 behind early second half, Gazza was then sent off, but a late Durie equaliser gave us our third draw of a campaign which yielded no victories, but we did play the eventual winners Juventus in our group who were a fantastic side.

I would imagine the quiet trip back to London was due to the cold and our adventures over the last few days taking their toll. My objective on our return was to make sure that we got our bounty deposit back from the ferry via Parks. Knowing that was unlikely as it was members money, I had to try. Despite written correspondence with Douglas Parks, it was a battle we could not win.

I could write like many others about various trips and the laughter and banter following Rangers. What makes these trips so special is our support, most if not nearly all of my closest friends I have met through travelling to games. Unfortunately some of these guys like Willie Muirhead, Nevil Balcombe and Brighton Dave are no longer with us, but still in our hearts. The trips now are more flights and occasionally by car, but even sweeter now as my son William travels with me and even my daughter Ailsa made the recent trip to Gibraltar.

@doubled1872

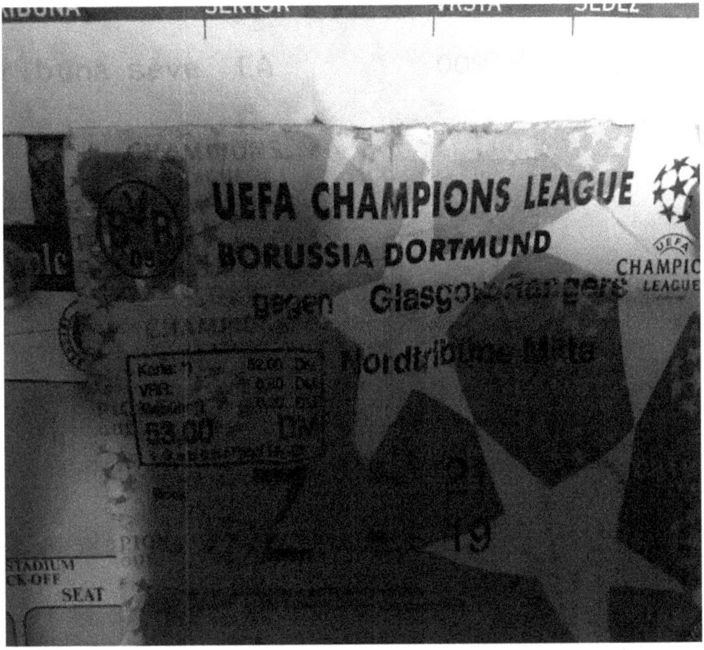
UEFA CHAMPIONS LEAGUE
BORUSSIA DORTMUND
gegen
SEAT

12: When John Greig tells you to keep the noise down, you listen!

FC Alania Vladikavkaz 2 v Rangers 7 – 21st August 1996 Champions League qualifying round, 2nd leg.

Story by: Robie Ferguson, Glasgow

We had to report to the Russian Consult in person a week before our trip. They asked us question about Rangers, where we worked and how much our salary was. Alastair Hood, Head of Security at Rangers had written to them, saying that the fans who were going were of good character and genuine supporters.

Monday 19th August 1996 – We set off from Glasgow, an early flight to Copenhagen. There was a difficult landing, so we were forty minutes late and we missed our connection to Stockholm and we got put on the next flight. We eventually got to Moscow airport, where we had to wait for four hours through customs and to collect our luggage. Eventually we got to our hotel in Moscow. About six or seven did not get their luggage, including me, due to not catching our Stockholm flight.

Tuesday 20th August – We had to get an early flight to Vladikavkaz from a different airport that we arrived in in Moscow. It was an air flop flight; unbelievable. There was a strong smell of diesel, people standing in the aisle and the lunch was a chicken leg and a cup of water. When we arrived in Vladikavkaz airport, we were straight on a bus and there were helicopters everywhere, as the war in Chechnya was only forty miles away. We arrived in our hotel, which was three stars. The Rangers team were also staying there. There were armed guards on every landing, pretty scary. We had to bring our own food, we were told by Rangers to do this. Six or seven of us did not get their luggage, me included. Thankfully, Walter Smith arranged for Jimmy Bell, Ranger kit man, to give us some Rangers gear; tops and shorts, to get us by. Once we settled into our hotel Walter Smith, Archie Knox, John Greig and Davie Dodds, came to the bar for a chat and we did an impromptu Q&A with them; it was a great laugh. We were advised not to leave the hotel at night as it was too dangerous. For once we listened!

Wednesday 21st August – Before the game, Rangers gave us free tickets; they were priced at $10. Some of the guys went down to the stadium in the afternoon for match programmes and were invited into the press box and were given a few free vodkas. We got the bus to the game and were joined by British Embassy staff from Moscow. We scored in the first minute and did not look back. I remember the locals shouting 'Glasgow Rangers', we were scoring at will; brilliant. McCoist got a hat trick, Laudrup got 2, Van Vossen got 1 and Charlie Miller got 1. At full time, the players came over to us; wee Durrant threw me his jersey, but it got stuck in the fence and a big Russian guy jumped up and got it on the other side of the fence. The goalie, Andy Goram saw it and gave me his and I have still got it to this day. I have been offered £500 for it, but no chance, I treasure it. After the game we all ended up in the tunnel with the players, wee Durranty promised me another top; Durranty has always been a great wee guy. Back at the hotel the guys had a few beers; some went to bed early and some stayed with the locals, who looked a bit dodgy – looked like mafia to me.

Thursday 22nd August – Early flight back to Moscow and again stayed in a hotel. Four of the guys got an early flight back, but this had to turn around back to Moscow, as there was a problem with the flight. Everyone was shattered; the guys who liked their booze were certainly shattered from all the Vodka; I had been teetotal for years.

Friday 23rd August – Flight back to Copenhagen. On the flight we learnt that we had drawn Ajax, Auxerre, Grasshoppers in the next round in the Champions League proper group stage. Then we had five hours until the flight home to Glasgow. No mobile phones in these days, so a couple of the guy's phoned home from airport to find that their pictures were on the back of the *Evening Times*. Two of the guys were not so pleased as they were supposed to be off work unwell. We arrived back late to Glasgow, a sleep and then off to see Rangers play Motherwell the next day.

A few other things that happened on the trip:
- First night at Vladikavkaz hotel, the guys were a bit rowdy, just singing Rangers songs. John Greig came down and asked us to be quiet as the players were trying to sleep.
- At the game Ian Archer, well known Journalist, was drunk and tried to get into the Russian end. Alastair Hood, Head of Security rescues him. I said to Hood, if that was one of us, you would want to take our season book off us.
- Brian Craig got Bjorklund's jersey, when drunk he said I will get buried in this shirt. The next game in Europe; Ajax away, he swapped it for a scabby Ajax t-shirt.
- We were all sitting outside the hotel in Vladikavkaz and Ally McCoist threw water down on us.
- When out in Moscow, we saw this queue a 100 yards long. Me being nosey, I wanted to see what it was. They were queuing for chocolate; they were so far behind the UK at this time. The next time I was in Russia it was much more Westernised.

«АЛАНИЯ»
Россия

96/97

«ГЛАЗГО РЕЙНДЖЕРС»
Шотландия

Республиканский стадион «Спартак» ● 21 августа 1996 года

HOTEL VLADIKAVKAZ

ФУТБОЛЬНЫЙ КЛУБ «АЛАНИЯ»
РЕСПУБЛИКАНСКИЙ СТАДИОН «СПАРТАК»
UEFA CHAMPIONS LEAGUE
ЛИГА ЧЕМПИОНОВ
КВАЛИФИКАЦИОННЫЙ РАУНД
СРЕДА 21 АВГУСТА 1996 ГОДА
Начало игры в 20.00
«АЛАНИЯ»
(Россия)
«ГЛАЗГО РЕЙНДЖЕРС»
(Шотландия)
ЗАПАДНАЯ ТРИБУНА
СЕКТОР
РЯД
МЕСТО
30
14
14
Стоимость билета 100 тысяч рублей

13: "I've had to block that Robert Duvall, he keeps phoning me"!

Bayer Leverkusen 1 v Rangers 2 – 22nd October 1998
UEFA Cup 2nd round 1st leg

Story by: David Scott, Blantyre nr Glasgow

I was brought up in Blantyre, near Glasgow. Ever since I can remember I've supported the Glasgow Rangers, as have, my big brothers Wullie and John, who were both Rangers daft and I just followed suit, it must have been genetic! Wullie took me to my first game on the David Livingstone supporter's bus. Most people will know David Livingstone was a famous explorer who discovered parts of Africa, the bus was named after this famous protestant Christian, Blantyre's most famous son. Although I was young, I remember Rangers were playing Clyde and we won 6 goals to 0. That was me hooked and I would pester our Wullie to take me to Ibrox anytime he could.

Leverkusen Away

As I got older, I attended the Rangers games myself. I was a member of the Blantyre Rangers supporters club and we left from a pub called Carrigans. We owned our own minibus and we decided it was time we ventured on our first European trip. Ten of us agreed; let us head over to Germany. As well as I, Andy McMillan, Scott McMillan, Alan Brown, Alex Forsyth, whose father Alex played for Rangers, David Morrison Snr, David Morrison Jnr, Davey Semple, Gupta and Der. Dick Advocaat was our new manager and he brought in some star players that season and we were expected to do well in the tournament. Our bus left Blantyre on the Monday night and we travelled through the night until we arrived at Dover. The ferry was bouncing, and the sing song was brilliant. From Calais we then travelled on to Cologne. We didn't have any digs booked as we just thought we would book a hotel when we got there. As a result, we ended up staying on a barge on the Rhine for 2 nights, which was brilliant and certainly different. The first night we were in a pub, a well-dressed man was sitting across from us and my mate said ' Hi Bob How are you doing' he said 'hello lads' and walked up the stairs in the bar. Scott said to us you call yourself Rangers fans and you don't know who he is. It turns out he was one of our Directors – Bob Brannan. We sent him up a round of drinks and 10 mins later he came back down the stairs and sat with us for a couple of hours. He asked us to come and meet him at the game and he got the media to take photos of our supporter's club flag 'Blantyre Rangers'. He also gave Scott his number and said keep in contact.

Rangers were brilliant that night and the star man was a young Barry Ferguson. I remember him dropping his shoulder and putting 4 Leverkusen players out the game. We scored 2 great goals, Van Bronckhorst and J Johansson scored that night. We had done our first European game and it was the first of many, we all got home safe with a great result.

Not long after we got home, Bob Brannan called Scott, and asked if the 10 of us would like to take part in a film called *A Shot at Glory*. The famous actor Robert Duvall who starred in the Godfather and our top scorer and Rangers legend, Ally McCoist, were in the movie. Of course, we all said yes and we got paid £35 per day. Some of the filming was in the old Rangers bar in Glasgow called Annie Millers, they gave us free lager all the time the filming was going on, but it was nonalcoholic. We also got the Blantyre Rangers flag in the film. It was partly filmed at Hampden Park and we had to get our faces painted red, white and blue, no hardship there. They asked us who was the loudest of us all and we said Alex Forsyth as he always was. Alex, being Alex, asked for more money for a speaking part – he has never changed over the years – but we let him away with it, as his old man played for the famous. The film was not the best, but at least we can say we did a film as Rangers fans. Since then, I've had numerous offers from Hollywood and had to block Robert Duvall on my phone, as he wouldn't give it a rest!

I am still a season ticket holder nowadays and I travel from Blantyre on the same supporter's bus, but now we leave from the Stonefield Tavern with all the same mates. We have added a few to our bus over the years, John Dunn and Davey McCormack, but the hard core are still there. We still display our Blantyre Rangers flag home and away when we can, and if the flag could talk it would have some great stories. My big brother Wullie passed away a couple of years ago, as I would have loved to have thanked him for taking me to my first game and making me a big blue nose. It's in our blood

LOYAL AND BLUE... Scott McMillan (centre, in black shirt) and his Blantyre mates enjoy some pre-match banter in Germany with Chief Executive Bob Brannan

either, they just chatted away about the game and about how we were enjoying the trip."

"It is very important that people in that kind of position don't forget that the fans are the most important part of the club

14: The Baillie Loyal on Tour

Bayern Munich 1 - Rangers 0
4th November 1999, Champions League

Story by: Helen Baillie – Kilwinning, Ayrshire

T'was a cold and grey November morn, when we left Inverness town haha, but seriously for some, the journey started the day before.

Jim and Mark and Evelyn Baillie left Bettyhill on the north coast of Scotland on Sunday 31st October to travel to Inverness, to meet up with Helen Baillie for a quick overnight, then board the Rapsons coach from The Portland Club at 5.30am Monday 1st November. Jim had every Rangers VHS in existence and was happy to take them along for the journey, a journey which lasted 5 days, with one overnight stop.

he Portland Club in Inverness was the departure point of choice, due to some amenable staff the club opened at 4am to allow travellers to use the facilities and stock up in any essentials that may have been overlooked – ice Vodka, slices of lemon etc, and of course as dedicated supporters of local business, a few quid was taken over the till, as the excitement built.

5.30am on the nose we left, our usual driver Graham at the helm, and a reserve driver 'Peter' in attendance. Peter did not seem overly enthused at my Dad's VHS collection and it was quite apparent why – caused a lot of hilarity during his driving stints when he was unable to change the VHS and was subjected to our the 9 in a row set on loop.

Spirits were high owing to the performances on the park and amount of actual spirits on the bus, this led to toilet levels being high and needing to be emptied before we even hit Aviemore (a grand total of 30 miles from our starting point).

Wish I had brought my wellies, was a phrase often heard after another paddling mission!

Our journey to Dover passed uneventfully, although service stations en-route were left flabbergasted by our arrival and perhaps not sorry to see us leave! Although, as with everywhere we visit, their tills felt the benefit of the blue pound.

At last we reached Dover, the ferry and a bit of freedom, a great opportunity to meet up with fellow travellers bound for Munich and swap stories of the journey so far. Unfortunately, a few members went down on the boat due to a particularly rough crossing, however most found that the alcohol consumed on the journey gave a sense of equilibrium, and a bouncy on the ferry ensued.

First stop off the Ferry – hypermarket to replenish stocks that had perished so far, meats and cheese obviously, as we were in France, after all.

Off to Stuttgart, we set with a rousing chorus of 'shat it in the war' for the French, and 'one world cup, two world wars'. These songs I was to learn were a staple when in France.

We arrived at the Ibis hotel in Stuttgart, slightly crumpled and definitely in need of a shower, after our first night spent on the bus in transit. It was like arriving in heaven; beer on tap, showers, a pool, beer on tap, food that didn't come out of plastic wrappers, and did I mention beer on tap?!

Chaos reigned on the assigning of rooms, finding of rooms, flags being unfurled and fisticuffs for who was getting a shower first. The more seasoned follower retired to the bar, confident that they would get a room and a shower at some point.

One little idiot amongst the trip – namely me – decided to use the downtime to dye my platinum blonde hair a deep shade of royal blue, looked awesome at the time – 3 months later not so much.

Off we set into Stuttgart to sample the local culture (beer) meet the locals (fellow drinkers) spread the blue pound (buy beer) and find somewhere to eat (drink beer).

We found a Rock bar that was empty, the owner opened up and the evening that ensued is best left unspoken about – what happens in Stuttgart, stays in Stuttgart, a rule that all away fans must follow.

The following morning there were no fresh faces to be seen, however it was match day – the reason for the trip, the famous Glasgow Rangers vs Bayern, in Germany. There was a real feeling we could get something from the game if not a victory, after the performance we put in against them at Ibrox in September.

A raucous breakfast ensued with the hotel staff counting down the minutes until our departure 3…….…..2……..….1.

Graham (the driver) came in for a word and a committee of men went outside, the bus wouldn't start. A very tense 8 hours ensued, friendships were tested and the air was blue, but huzzah the bus was fixed and we were finally on our way.

As we neared the stadium the excitement really built up to a frenzy, with 40 odd bears desperate for release. Owing to the time, we went directly to the stadium, and I have never in my life felt an adrenalin spike like it. We had all been home and away domestically, but this was our first European Away trip and it was the moment the Rangers Family really hit home to me – we walked in and our flags and banners were laid out along the track and everywhere we looked there were happy smiling faces, swapping the stories of their travels, helping out those in need, and really demonstrating what it is to be part of the Rangers Family.

The game overall was an anti-climax and the devastating injury sustained by our own Michael Mols will never be forgotten, and we do still wonder what might've been.

The journey home as with all return journeys was a bit of a blur, however for each and every one of us it would prove to not be the last trip and we enjoyed many more journeys with ITBs and some as Baillie Loyal exclusives. We would encourage anyone with the opportunity to follow Rangers away in Europe, it truly defines the Rangers Family.

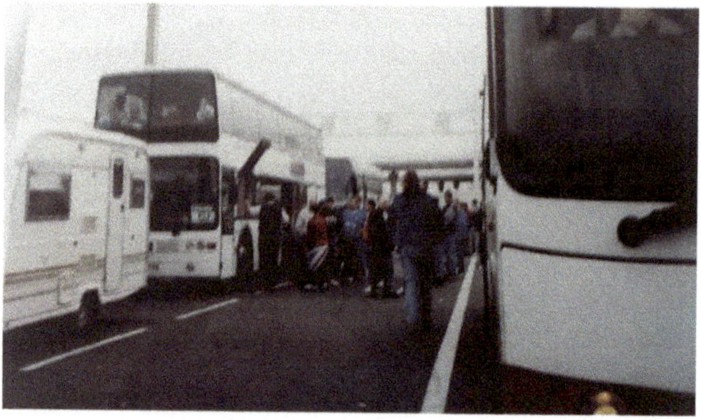

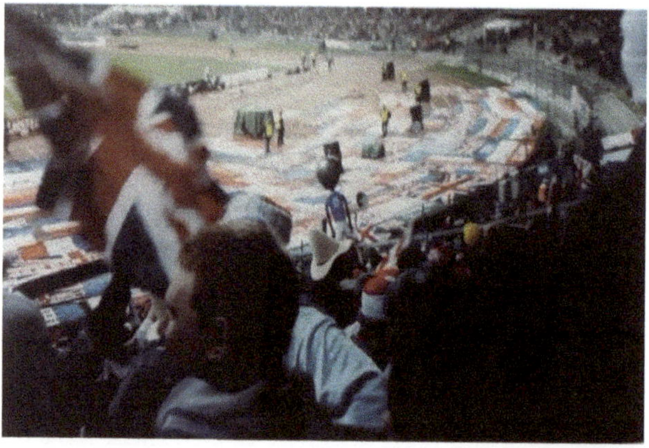

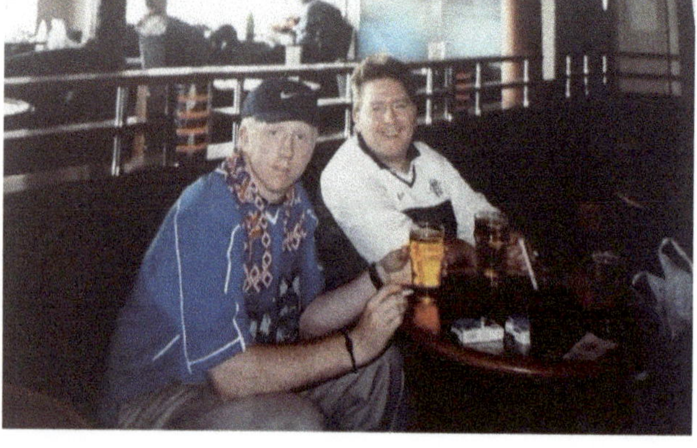

15: 'Haw Batman, whit ur you daein'

Borussia Dortmund 2 Rangers 0
(Dortmund won on pens after Rangers won 1st leg 2-0)
9.12.99 – UEFA Cup 3rd round 2nd leg

Story by : Brian Matthews Glasgow Oswald's Bar

We had just played in the Champions League against Bayern Munich in 1999 and we were very unlucky to get beaten, not helped by the horrendous injury to Mikey Mols. However, we were still on a high going into the UEFA cup at the time and we drew Dortmund. At Ibrox we won 2-0, one of those famous nights under the floodlights. Our next game was away to Dortmund, and Germany is always popular with the troops, so there were thousands of us, still on a high. We thought there was a wee chance here, we'll skate it, all we need is to get a draw or get beaten 1-0, but in a tough game they beat us 2-0, it went to penalties and Rangers sadly lost.

However, as always, the trip had some highlights. When we got to Dortmund, thousands were arriving in Germany by all means of transport. We arrived a couple of nights before the match, just to acclimatise. We were all going out, hundreds of Rangers fans along the main drag and we saw these big billboards; 'live sex show'. Everybody had gone, we needed to go to this, you know some of them (none of my mates obviously), go to brothels, but we just wanted to have a laugh and go to a live sex show. We steamed in and it was like any other cinema, like you would get in Glasgow, all the seats up at an angle. There was a stage at the front, and we were mingled in with the local Germans, everybody all just mingled in, so we piled in where we could get a few seats together. How romantic eh?! The next thing we know the lights go off and the Batman tune comes on, I thought what the hell is going on here. Then the curtains open and there is this damsel in distress, she is like 'ahhhh ahhhh' and she had the Joker sort of roughing her up a wee bit. The next thing we know, this great big black man dressed as Batman comes on to save her. We've did a bit of cheering and clapping. Batman takes his gear off and in this case it's definitely not true what they say about black guys, it was tiny, so we were heckling him. Batman is a wee Robin, was the cry from us. Batman then wrestles the Joker, gets him out the way, starts to have sex and shags this damsel in distress on this big stage in front of the audience. Then there is a big cheer and during this all I here is, "Oh what the fuck", so I thought what is going on here and then I hear "what the fuck are you doing here" from the other side. There was a big commotion going on in all different parts of the cinema and I thought what is going on here, this is nuts. I turn to the right and one of the German guys was beside me and he had got a long jacket on and they were all having a ham shank under those long jackets. Myself and a couple of the boys were saying "Errr what the fuck you dirty bastard". I grabbed this German and all other Rangers fans were grabbing the Germans and dragging them out. There was a pile of Germans outside with their cocks out of their jackets. The Rangers boys are going mental, saying "ya dirty perverts". Then we all piled back into the show and said "right Batman carry on, as you were." We are sitting cheering Batman and the next thing you know all the lights come on and the Police come in. However, someone must have explained to them that we thought the Germans are dirty perverts and they explain to us, no that is the done thing round here. They told us these guys all have these big jackets and they all come to watch the show wearing them, it is a given. After all the drama Batman couldn't get a hard on so we weren't popular, so that was it. Next night I got my long coat on and went back myself for batman part 2!

Their stadium was different class, it kept the noise in, it was hair on the back of the neck stuff, their fans were going mad, they were allowed flares and the pyrotechnics, which was new to me back then. I think that part of the stadium behind the goals it is called the Yellow Wall and it's an impressive sight.

I have been abroad about 8 times I think, an amateur compared to many I know. I've done the old skool Rangers supporters' bus to Europe; I think it was 34 hours and it is alright going as you are bouncing but see if you get beat; it is a long journey back!

My very first ever Rangers game was the Battle of Britain, Leeds. I was hooked after that.

I now own 2 Rangers bars, Oswald's in Glasgow city centre and my new one just about open at time of going to print (Covid permitting) Lounge 72 in Rutherglen. If you are near either pop in for a drink, you will get a warm welcome.

@Brian_Glow

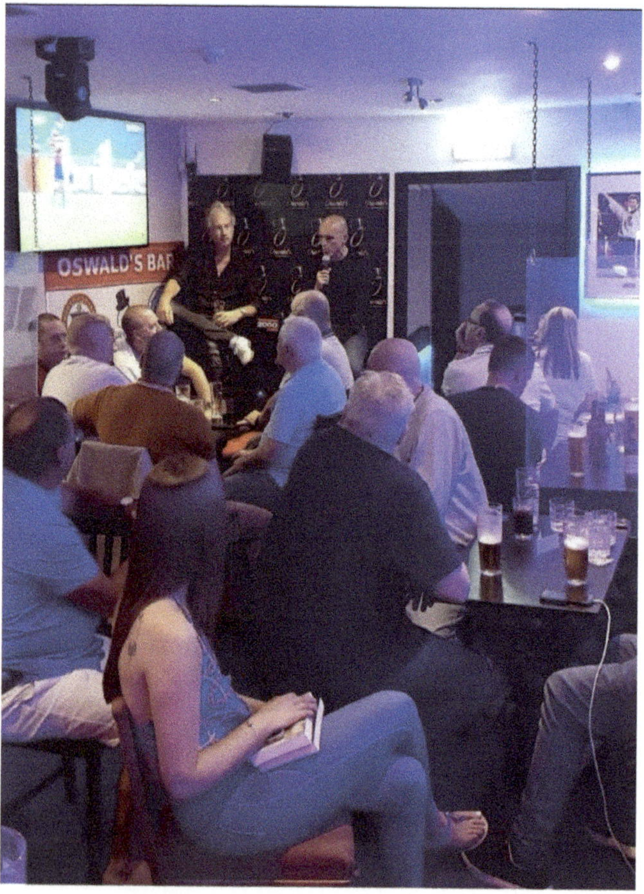
OSWALD'S BAR

16: Aki's Tours To Maribor

Maribor 0 v Rangers 3 – Champions League Qualifier 2nd Round 1st Leg, 25th July 2001

Story by: Akram 'Aki' Mohammed, Larkhall

For as long as I can remember I have followed Glasgow Rangers. I was brought up in Harthill, so there was always going to be only one team for me. A big part of my life has been going to watch the famous Glasgow Rangers. I am now a season ticket holder in the member's suite hospitality. I am also proud to have a blue room in my Indian restaurant, Spice in Hamilton, just along from the racecourse

Going to European away games has always been a big part of being a Rangers fan for those fortunate enough to be able to travel abroad. Over the years I have regularly booked flights for up to 30 of my mates for European games and they were nicknamed 'Aki's Tours'. I remember we were going to a game in Lisbon with the boys and we had around 40 on the flight. As per norm, the crack on the flight was great. I wasn't drinking or eating due to Ramadan. My mates were taking the piss, as they were getting merrier and I was stone called sober. The stewardess then came up with the drinks trolley and I asked for a double Drambuie. All my mates were cheering and asking me how come you are having a drink when it's Ramadan. I joked, it doesn't count if you are 3,000 feet up in the air. The whole plane was in stitches of laughter.

So, when we drew Maribor in the cup, as you can imagine at that time, it was not the easiest place to get to. To be honest, most of us had never heard of Maribor. We agreed a plan to travel to Trieste, it was a wee town on the border between Italy and Slovenia. Our journey started with us flying from Prestwick to Stansted, and from Stansted to Trieste. The first obstacle we had happened in Prestwick. Some of us decided to have a game of golf at Royal Prestwick in the morning and by the time we got to the airport, as usual Ryanair had overbooked the plane. There were ten of us, they said that five of us could get on the plane and five couldn't. We said, but we have got another flight to catch at Stansted to get us to Trieste, so we weren't happy and were pleading our case. But they weren't moving, classic nothing we can do patter, the plane was overbooked. Then suddenly they came up with an idea. They said listen, the one thing we can do for you, everybody is on the plane, so we can make an announcement, that you can offer £50 each for five people go come off and they can get the next flight to Stansted. Have you ever heard anything like that before in your life? We are having to pay extra because of their greed!

They made an announcement and we had to give £50 each to give to five folks to come off the plane. To our surprise and delight, these five people agreed to do this, saying it wasn't a bother to get another plane, £50 to wait at Prestwick for another hour.

A result for us. We were on our way to Stansted to get a flight to Trieste. The 2nd flight to Trieste was a dawdle. When we got out there, we were thinking we will get a few hire cars, but we were in a middle of nowhere so we had to get hold of a minibus and a driver. The driver was great, he spoke decent English and drove us out of Trieste on the day of the game to Maribor. The minibus was only a 9-seater, so it was a driver and 8, and there were 10 of us. Therefore, as you do, we took 2 chairs out of the hotel and put them in where the luggage goes at the back. We were off!

We were driving an hour or so out to the Slovenian border and next thing, our driver tells us he can't take 2 of us over the border as he will get fined. Plan B, two of the boys had to get out and walk over the border and get back in the taxi on the other side, once we were through. Mission accomplished without any hiccups. It was Maribor, here we come.

It was a good wee journey, stopping off at a couple of bars. We got to Maribor and headed towards the main square, and if you remember Maribor at that time, it wasn't on many tourist maps. But it was brilliant, the sun was shining, the Bears were in town and it was cheap as chips. We are partying away in a wee bar and the songs are being sung.

However, it is time to head to the game. After the game it's back to the bar and the wee lassie who ran the bar was so grateful to see us. She said she took more in a day, than she would in 3 months! We bought even more beer for the minibus for on the way back and we still had wads of this money to spend, it was just unreal.

Then on the way back, by this time everybody is rocking and the songs are being sung. Before we know it the two boys had to get off again at the border and the guy says to him, where is it you are going and he says Glasgow. In the middle of the border between Italy and Slovenia and the boys say we are going to Glasgow and they were on foot. The border security guy just shook his head and waved the boys through.

In terms of the game, we had a strong team, including, Tore André Flo, Caniggia and Reyna, we won 3-0 comfortably. There probably were about 1,000 Rangers fans there, not bad in July and it wasn't the easiest place to get to.

Over the years I have gone with the Club, in the Team plane but in general we always travel by ourselves, with 'Akis Tours'

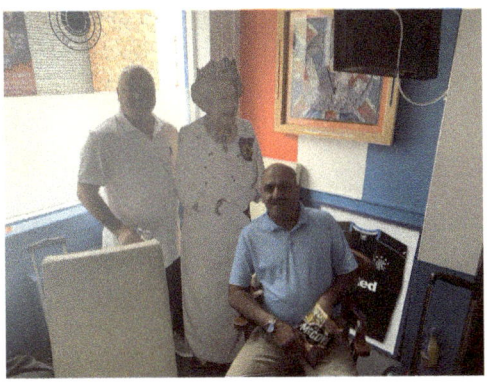

17: Caledonia to Catalonia

Barcelona 2 v Rangers 0
7th November 2007 – Champions League

Story by: Roddy Maclean – Inverness True Blues

My first Rangers game was Aberdeen v Rangers at Pittodrie in 1969. The game ended in a 0-0 draw, but what a thrill to see the likes of John Greig and Orjan Persson. In 1972, aged 16 and living in Inverness, it wasn't common to go to places like Barcelona for a European Final. I listened to the game on the radio, as it was not on live TV. The match was shown later that night in black and white. Two weeks before the Barcelona game, Rangers played an Inverness Select team in a Highland League ground; just a few minutes walk from my house, with Rangers winning 5-2, I remember it like it was yesterday.

On a side note, one of the 'Barca Bears' Willie Mathieson, ended up staying in Inverness for several years and was a great ambassador for Rangers, who I got to know well. Willie was a humble man and would regularly come to functions that we were having for the supporter's club. During this time, he gave me a poster advertising the 1972 European Cup Winners Cup final, that was signed by the whole team from that night. The supporter's club still treasure it to this day.

As that was Rangers third European Final in 11 years, I told myself "I will get to the next one", obviously not anticipating then that I would have to wait forty years until Rangers played Zenit St Petersburg in 2012.

Around 1971, a group of us started travelling to games with a local Rangers Supporters Club. The long day would begin with us leaving Inverness at 7am. We would take in the game and then go to the Wee Rangers Club, usually getting the last Subway to Buchanan Street Bus Station, where the bus for Inverness left at midnight, getting us back to Inverness for 5am the next day. Away games in those days were easier to get to, as the grounds had a much bigger capacity than they do now and tickets for away games were easier to get your hands on.

The supporters club I began travelling with was called Inverness Rangers Supporters club, which eventually evolved into the Inverness True Blues. As the years rolled, I was tasked with running this supporters club and organised buses to all home and away games including Europe. Some stories there, I can tell you. As flying to games started to get popular, we started going with Myles from Sports Options. We would fly with them but made our own way to the airport, usually Glasgow, to catch our plane.

Upon drawing Barcelona in the group stages of the Champions League in 2007, we were in no doubt we would be part of the 20,000 or so, Rangers fans that made the invasion. As we began to discuss the options on how to get there, we realised that there was a huge interest and talked about the possibility of running our own plane from Inverness.

I spoke to Sports Options and the only plane they could get for us was a 240-seater jet, but they queried if we would be able to get enough people going to even partly fill it and make it viable. Well, we filled the plane easily and I believe it was the biggest passenger jet to fly from Inverness. The morning of departure at the airport, was a sight to behold. The gate for checking in was queued out of the doors of the airport, the likes of which has not been seen very often at Inverness Airport.

I personally knew everybody on this trip, a few were even in Barcelona in 1972. So off we flew to Barcelona, to play arguably the best team in the world, who we had held to a 0-0 draw just a fortnight prior, at Ibrox. Ronaldinho, Messi & Co. had been held in check by the likes of Alan Hutton on that occasion but ended up running out 2-0 winners on the return leg.

Nevertheless, we were not bothered about the score, we were simply happy to be there following the Rangers. We had 3 days and 2 nights in a four-star hotel which was magic. The whole time we were there was brilliant, being amongst so many Rangers fans from all over the world and soaking up the atmosphere in the build up to the game. Nearly everybody on the plane had tickets, the few that did not, eventually got sorted with tickets for the match soon after landing in Barcelona, which was great.

Time flew by though and before we knew it, it was time to leave Barcelona and head back to the Highlands. Gaining an hour back due to the time difference meant that we were back in the Portland Club, the former base of our supporter's club, having a pint by 17:30. It was quicker than it would normally take us to travel up the A9 from Glasgow to Inverness on a regular match day. Many people could not believe we had been at the game and chartered a plane to go there. Mind you, the welcoming home committee from the police was over the top, when we came back. While queuing at passport control, we were accompanied by two police dogs, 8 police officers and an inspector. Some welcome home, eh?

I still run the supporters club and I am proud to be a True Blue. My wife's grandfather, Robert Bolt, played for Rangers between 1939-1945.

Keeping up the family traditions, all four of my children and most of my grandchildren have been season ticket holders at Ibrox.

Hopefully, we will get to make it to another European final someday soon. In the meantime, myself and the Inverness True Blues will enjoy 55.

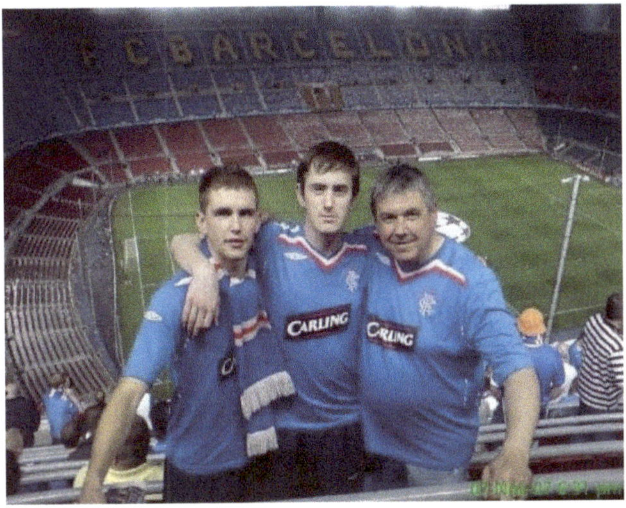
CARLING
CARLING

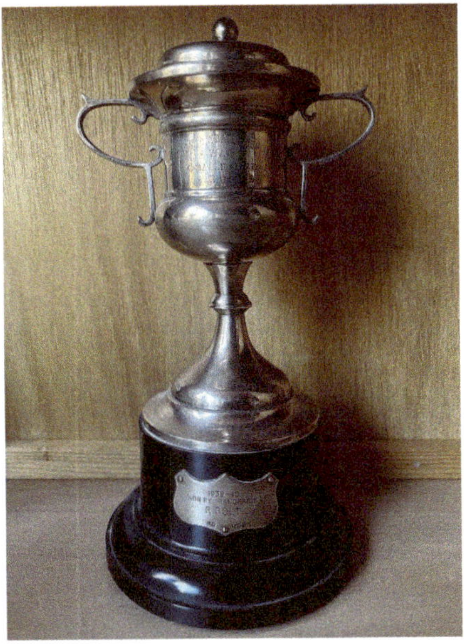

18: Flying the Flag in France

**Lyon 0 v Rangers 3, 3rd October 2010
Champions League**

Story by: Wilf Marshall, Aberdeen

On this trip I went with three guys from up here in Aberdeen. The funny thing about the three guys I was with, was that one of them had been away for 4 years' working in Saudi, had come back and decided he was coming with us, one does not go to a lot of games, but he goes to all the European away games and the other one is like myself and never misses a game at all. We left from Aberdeen, flew down to London, then from there across to Lyon with no hiccups en route for once. The strange thing about it though, it was the first and only time we checked our bags in for a European game. It was because the guy who had worked in Saudi had got a huge flag made for us, so we thought we would have to check that in. As we got to Lyon we are walking through the baggage hall and his name got announced, and informed his bag was still in London! In itself that would not have been a problem, but the guy has got a false eye, all his eye drops were in the bag, so that was a bit of an issue for him, to say the least. It is just ironic that it was the first and only time we had checked a bag in and it went missing. However, they delivered it to the hotel the next morning, so problem solved, back to focussing on the game and getting to know Lyon.

It was the day before the game and we were in Lyon in the afternoon. It was actually quite subdued the night before and we are thinking, where are all the other Bears? Lyon is beautiful, absolutely beautiful. We were kicking about the old town, it was really nice and we walked into the pub and the only folk in this pub, it was late on, were three or four other

Rangers fans and that was it, there was nobody else. One of them was a guy with his head shaved and his hair was in the shape of two horns at the side of his head. He was wearing a Rangers away top (on the back of it he had Satan 666) and the punk tartan trousers with the chains on them. The guy is apparently a Social Worker from the Black Isle and it is the first time I ever met him. They were cracking company and that is all I can remember from the night before the game!

As we always like visiting stadiums before games, and as our hotel was only half a mile from the stadium, we went over and tried to get in. Unfortunately, they were having none of it, saying there is no way that you are getting in. There was a big steward and although his English was better than our French, it wasn't great, and he said look you can't get in and he predicted a score with his fingers which was 3-0. I said, yes okay mate, au revoir. Much to our amusement, I saw him after the game and I said you were right, but it wasn't the 3-0 that you meant, hard luck pal. So that was the night before and then obviously the day of the game, we were just in the square with all the bears having a party. As always, it was a great atmosphere bumping into familiar faces. It was decent weather and then we headed down to the ground quite early, before all the shenanigans and all the daft stuff starts. Although there were not as many dafties there as were sometimes and can be now. We were sitting in the square just having a drink with some of our pals and The Goalie (Andy Goram) appeared, as he tended to do. I am sure that was the trip when he told me that he never, ever goes to the game and said to me, 'I go all the trips, love all the crack with the guys but I never go to the game because I am bad luck.'

So, we went down to the game and we went up to the top tier to stick up the banner which, by this time had appeared. We had to hang it off the top tier because the thing was massive. The game was incredible. It was memorable for the first goal, because Rangers were shooting towards us in the first half, we got the corner, my mate Martyn, the one with the dodgy eye, as soon as the ball was in flight, he just turned round to me and he said GOAL and he was celebrating the goal while the ball was still on the cross. This was because you could just see where it was going and it was in the back of the net. 1-0, Lee McCulloch. It was bedlam, absolute bedlam and I turned round and two of my mates were now two rows behind us and I turned round to celebrate with them and the next thing I knew I was flying above them. I was crowd surfing, my legs were taken from me and I was crowd surfing, it was just incredible. It was just absolutely incredible. That was probably the best European bouncy bouncy's we ever had by the way. The second was scored by Cousin and Beasley got the third one in on a breakaway. They hit the post and bar about three times, they did everything but score. The thing I always remember about the game over there, they brought on a Scottish Piper and he pitched up with Broxi Bear and that was quite good crack with him and Broxi bouncing about, that was a good laugh.

Obviously after the game we headed away, back up towards the hotel. Halfway between the stadium and our hotel there was a place, it was Olympic Lyon Café. We had popped in during the day and it was quiet and there was a life size cut out of Juninho on the wall, you know because he was their big superstar at the time. So, after the game we walked back up and one of the boys said, 'shall we just pop in here' because we didn't want to go all the way into town as we were near the hotel, so we said we would hang about there, as it was the only place, we could find that was open. To our amusement it was full of pissed off French men, but they could not have been nicer.

We were in there for a good hour after the game which was a good laugh. Then we headed back down to the ground to see if we could get a look at it and finally got a look at it. We had noticed that at the back of the ground there was a dual carriageway and at the side of this, we noticed there was a layby. In the layby were four transit vans, and on the dashboard of each of the vans, there was a tray with tea light candles on it and sitting in the passenger seat was basically a hooker. So, these hookers are in transit vans and as we walked past one of them, the side door opened and there was a bed in the back of it. So, it was like mobile hookers, it was unbelievable. Well, we thought, we have got to get a photo of this. So one of us took a photo and the flash goes off, the hooker gets out and starts chasing us up the street. Schoolboy error!

Certainly, a bit different from my first European away v Bohemians in Dublin, in '84. That was mental. That was horrendous. The furthest that I have travelled so far to watch Rangers is Tel Aviv.

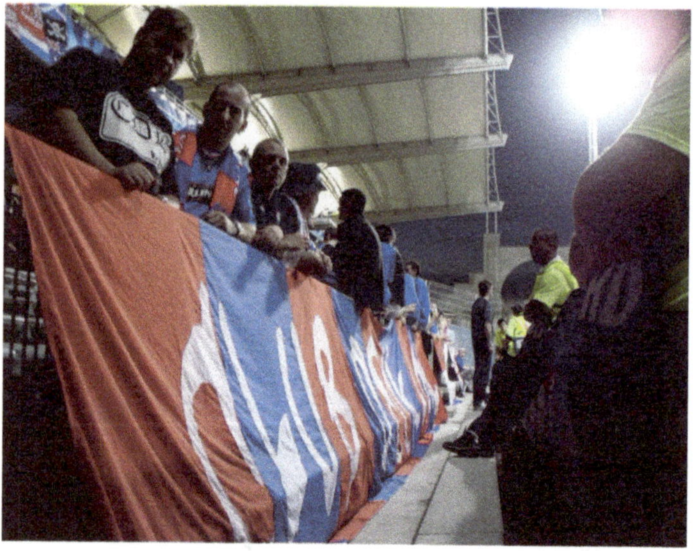

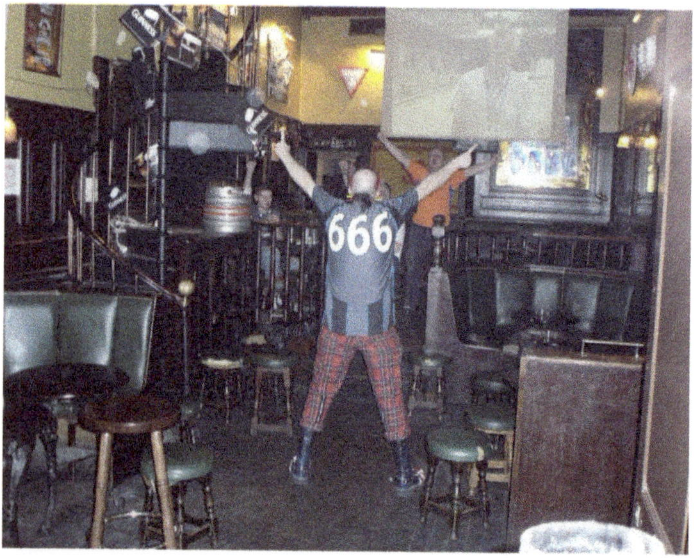
666

19: Snowballing at the Acropolis in February

Panathinaikos 1 - Rangers 1,
Athens, 21st February 2008, UEFA Cup

Story by: Ronnie Hughes & Fiona Desmond
(The Studham Loyal)

When the Champions League and UEFA Cup draws were made on 14th December 2007, Ronnie and I couldn't quite believe it, our beloved teams Rangers and Chelsea were both playing in the same city, in the same week, we were counting the days until February! It's always a challenge to get good deals for Euro trips as the airlines and hotels are way too savvy these days! Miraculously, on Expedia, we got a week's holiday – flight and hotel for £150 each, flying British Airways from Heathrow on the Sunday before the game. Heathrow is half an hour from where we live! The hotel ended up being a bit of a dive, but we didn't care!

Finally, February came, and we were enjoying a few wines on our flight to Athens, when the pilot announced over the PA, that we were diverting to Rhodes as Athens airport had been closed due to heavy snow, **snow**? This was Greece, not Russia or Norway! Apparently, snow had not shut Athens airport for 70 odd years. We thanked our lucky stars we were with British Airways and not a low-cost airline, as we were so well looked after and lapped up the fact that we were put up in a 5 star hotel in Rhodes Town for the night, buckshee. Lots of our fellow passengers were moaning about the inconvenience, but we embraced it and saw it as an adventure, taking advantage of a wee bar crawl around Rhodes Town, before hitting the hotel bar until late, in the company of a few football fans from north and south of the border.

The Rangers game wasn't until the Thursday, so we were pretty hopeful of making it. We later heard about Bears who had been forced to take all sorts of weird and wonderful routes to get to Athens, as their flights from the UK had been cancelled due to bad weather. Some flew to Italy and took a ferry to Patras in Greece and then took a 3-hour bus ride to Athens, forking out hundreds of pounds for their efforts. Thankfully, we were on a flight to Athens the following day and we arrived early afternoon. Some of our pals were already there and had found a pub of choice which we used as our main base for the next few days. It became a Rangers/Chelsea bar and the staff made us very welcome. The landlord even asked us to help him with his coupon! So many people were talking about their nightmare journeys to Athens and this ended up being a great way to get to know people we hadn't met before. One of the guys, Millsy, from Kent, had a ticket for the Chelsea game on the Tuesday and was desperate for a ticket for the Rangers game, he had booked to stay in Athens for a week, on the off chance he could pick up a ticket for Thursday's game too. Ronnie and I had bought our tickets through the Rangers ticket office, but Millsy was in the right place at the right time – earlier that day we had been drinking with pals from the Edinburgh Union Jack, who knew of a spare ticket which we bought and passed it to Millsy, he was over the moon! We had never met him before and we've ended up being great pals.

By the Wednesday, Athens was over-run with Rangers and Chelsea fans and we all got together to watch **them** v Barca that evening. No prizes for guessing who we were supporting and Messi and Henry didn't disappoint. By the end of the evening any of the neutrals in the bars knew who we were!

On the morning of the game some of our group saw the players casually strolling round the Acropolis, but we had to stay in the boozer as Ronnie had the sh*ts! I thought it was a poor excuse from Ronnie, why didn't he just say he wanted to stay in the square on the bevvy enjoying the pre match build up, that's normal behaviour on a Rangers Euro trip, right? It was a scorching hot day, and the humidity was unreal, so we all had to keep ourselves hydrated, so it made sense so stay near to the watering holes. The main square was packed with Bears and carry outs and Rangers flags adorned every tree, doorway and balcony. I'm not sure how many Bears actually made it to the stadium as there seemed far more in the square that day than attended the game!

The Police started rounding up the Rangers fans early afternoon to get us to the game, but we thought it was far too early, so we disappeared to a bar around the corner in the company of many familiar Gers and Chelsea faces. The Police eventually wised up to this and used "unnecessary force" to get us onto trains to the Apostolos Nikolaidis Stadium. Apparently, it is the oldest stadium in Greece, no kidding! If it were in the UK, it would have been demolished planets ago!

The journey to the game was as expected, herded like cattle by overzealous Police with ferocious dogs, who looked like they hadn't eaten for weeks and had probably been promised Bears for their dinner. We were in high spirits and fine voice regardless, a few "jobsworths" in uniform aren't going to spoil our fun! I wondered why there was netting over the top of the away section and when I saw the hostility of the home fans, it was pretty obvious. We were bombarded with all sorts of missiles and plastic cups of urine. There was a home fan with his face pressed against the segregation barrier wearing a Celtic top and goading us, not one of his better ideas, as he would no doubt find out later. One of the Bears, Billy Farmer, saw a guy wearing a pink suit (yes, pink!) in an area with Rangers Directors and other dignitaries and he was taking a pounding with chants of "who's the salmon in the pink".

When we saw the team news, we thought Walter was really going for it, opting for Boydy and Novo up front, instead of his preferred 4-5-1 formation in Europe. After a dismal 0-0 home tie the week before, he had to change something! Unfortunately, the home team were more up for it than Rangers and we conceded early on. The first half was a lacklustre performance from Rangers, the away fans were displaying more energy and enthusiasm than the 11 guys in blue on the park! Thankfully, McGregor made a couple of fine saves and we went in only 1-0 at the break, having missed some good chances ourselves. In the second half, the Greens continued to dominate the game and Walter brought on Steven Naismith for Papac and Christian Dailly for Adam after 65 minutes, in what we hoped and prayed would be a game changer, as time was now running out. Just when it felt like we were dead and buried and out of Europe, Novo found the ball at his feet and did what he does so well and buried it in the bottom left corner. Cue mental celebrations in the away end for the rest of the game and all through the extra time we had to stay in the stadium before we could leave, delighted that we were through to the last 16 of the Uefa Cup, as well as still in contention for 3 other trophies.

Back to the square we all went to continue the party, pondering who we would get in the next round. Later that evening, we bumped into a pal from Glasgow, Andy Cumming, who ended up in one of the more "up market bars" in the square and he got chatting to some German guys at the bar, who asked him if he had been at the game. "Aye, I sure was," Andy said with a smile on his face wider than Loch Ness. Andy then asked the German guy if he had seen the game and he said yes, he was the referee! Andy and his pals had a great chat to Felix (Brych) and the other guys with him, who he assumed were the rest of the match officials. The bars stayed open until the last Bear standing and we went back to our hotel very pleased we were still in Europe, but not before walking through a wee game of Bears versus the local skateboarders, chucking oranges at each other.

We managed to do some of the tourist stuff the day we went home, before going back to the boozer to watch Soccer Saturday, where the main story was of a young Eduardo of Arsenal suffering that horrendous leg break at St Andrews. We had an uneventful journey home compared to some; Billy Farmer's flight back to Glasgow straight after the game wasn't much fun at all, the landing was aborted **twice** due to freezing fog!

So, onto Sunday's game at home to Gretna, four points clear at the top of the table, the CIS Cup Final to look forward to, as well as still in contention for the FA Cup and the UEFA Cup. Who knows how the season would finish for us?

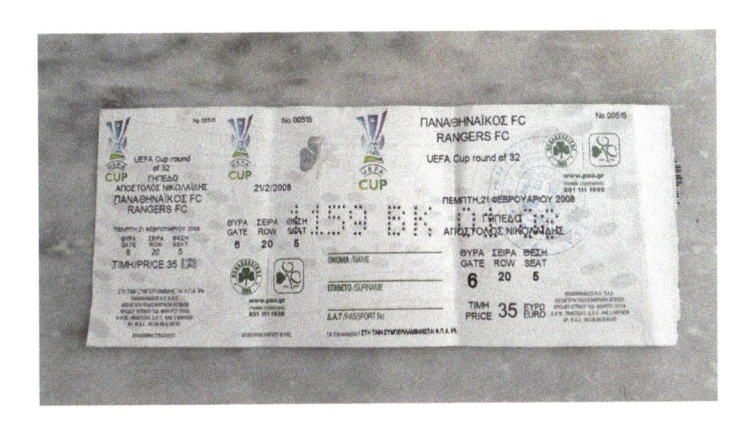

20: 'Pass the ball Whittaker'

Sporting Lisbon 0 v Rangers 2, 10th April 2008
Europa League Quarter Final
Story by: Allan Galbraith West Sussex

I was born and bred in Port Glasgow, but I'm now living down the south of England. Ever since I was a wee boy, it was always Rangers 1st in my house. It was not until I was about 9 that I realised the extent of this. One day playing football, I looked over to see if my Dad had seen the crunching tackle that I had just made. There he was, standing with a radio next to one of the other dads- shouting at it like a mad man. Rangers were only playing Dundee. Thankfully, that was engraved into me and is still present to this day. Through the rubbish years that we have all had, Rangers gives us something to look forward to every week. You can follow some of my journey on Twitter @GlasgowIsBlue72 where I engage with fellow bluenoses, when I'm not being ran ragged by a two-year-old bluenose of my own.

In my chosen away v Sporting Lisbon in 2008, Rangers needed a win to progress into the semi- final and somehow my mate and I managed to get a couple of tickets. As I watched the first leg down in Greenock, it was always going to be difficult and nerve racking – going over to Portugal to get the result and progress. We managed to get a quick couple of days over there, flying out on the day of the game. Now, I am not the best at flying, but after a few wee drams, I'm good. First thing in the morning, we are at the airport. Breakfast and beer, that's the only thing that's on my mind. We get on the plane, there are a few bluenoses scattered around – one guy already absolutely hammered and trying to do the bouncy with his seat belt on, here we, go it's off to the match we go! We land, my mate is absolutely hammered already and loving life.

I'm standing looking for a pub as I need to get on his level. We get in a taxi; my mate tells the guy where we are going. About 15 mins later, (This is you) said the taxi guy. Buzzing, we jumped out! My mate starts singing Follow Follow, whilst I ask him where the feck is it? I ask the taxi guy, where is the stadium? Stadium? He said to me. Yes, football stadium. "oh, that's not far from here, Jose Alvalde". Yes mate, that is what we need! The guy had taken us to an Aldi somewhere, but it was not a wasted trip. We got some cheap dodgy beer whilst we were there. We got set up in our digs – not far from the stadium. After that, we took a wee walk up towards the stadium. I did not believe that was the stadium at first, it looked like something from Minecraft. There was a nice wee bit of grass down from the stadium, next to a road that we sat on with a few cans and our flag on the grass. We ended up in some wee bar and got talking to another Rangers guy who was on crutches. He told us how he nearly did not make it but could not say no. He was there with a few other lads and a girl – they were bringing him drinks as he was sitting with his leg on a chair. We had a few, it was chilled out at this point.

Fast forward – nerves kicked in! Off we went up into the tier in the stadium – the Fans were right up for this! Kick off approaching, Rule Britannia bursts out then another song, then another song. The teams came out, we erupted! To be honest, you could not hear a thing from the Sporting end, as our support just kept singing their heart out. Sporting were doing well and at times, I thought they were going to score and end our hopes. We managed to get into the break 0-0; usually at half time everybody is chilled, talking away and having a munch. We were all too nervous, and the only way to beat it was to keep singing. The teams came out for the second half, we were bouncing again. Not long after, we went in front! Unbelievable, limbs everywhere, drinks everywhere – we were on our way to the semi-final. I was thinking, this is going to be the longest half an hour of my life now. We are going to sit back and defend as they needed to score two goals now. Not sure whether to cry, laugh, sing, or just not look.

Rangers make the changes; Whittaker comes on the field now. Jesus Christ Steven do not mess this up! Sporting are pressing to get a goal but we keep holding firm. Then the unbelievable happens! We intercept, and there is your man Steven Whittaker on the ball, running up the pitch. Go on son! Go on son! Pass it, pass it!! F****** PASS IT STEVEN! No way, SHOOT SHOOT. Boom goal... Yaaaaaaaasssssssss. The place erupts that is it- we are in the semi-final. Remember the guy on crutches from earlier? The guy that couldn't walk to the bar?. Well, I look down, and there he is bouncing up and down with his crutches in the air. I thought, he's going to need a few paracetamols in the morning. After the full-time whistle, we all stayed there and cheered the team when they came over. I stood with my hands on my head watching everybody go crazy and watching the team applaud us all. It just felt like a surreal moment for what he had just achieved.

We had done well up to that game, probably because our defending was like a brick wall – but it does not, it is getting the result that counts. A few had us written off going to Portugal and progressing, but in true Rangers style, we did it. But one thing during that trip that will always stick out in my mind. There was a man, probably around his 60's, who was homeless. He was offering to draw wee pictures to take home for a small price. He had a wee hat that people would put money in to and he had a few coins in there. By that night, that hat was full of money that Rangers fans had given him. Also, not 100% sure what the food place was called, but the Rangers fans kept buying food and giving it to the guy and he literally had a stack of takeaway food and drinks there to keep him going for about a month – he did not have to worry about eating for the next few weeks anyway. That is one thing I'll always take away from that trip, the true generosity of the famous.

@GlasgowIsBlue72

Sporting-Rangers

Só eles sabem porque não ficaram em casa

Cautelas atr... deram frutu...

«Este resultado não tem justificação»

«Tentaremos ir o mais longe possível»

21: 'The Ulsterman's match day'
Story by: Tim Webb, Portadown, Northern Ireland

Born a Ranger, and in 1993/94, I guess around the age of 4 or 5 years old, I started to go to home games at Ibrox. It has since progressed to semi finals and finals, but as regards league and cup games for previous rounds in the cup competitions, I try to get over to every home game. It was between my Dad and my late Uncle Denver, who got me started attending games.

I now sit in the East Enclosure and in particular, the wheelchair area of the East Enclosure and my seat/space is roughly 5 yards from the home dugout. I moved to there from my old seat/space which was in the West Enclosure, but that particular seat/space was right in the corner and I couldn't really see much. When the chance came available to move, I requested the move and thankfully the request was accepted by Rangers.

I start a match day with getting up at the early hour of 4:15am, with the help of both my Mum and Dad. I am then helped into the car by my Dad, who drives the car over to Ibrox. The journey consists of a few pickups along the way towards the boat terminal for the 7:30am sailing across from Larne to Cairnryan. We arrive at the stadium by about 11:45am. On return, we get the 8pm sailing from Cairnryan back to Larne and get back home for roughly 11pm that night. It's a long day, but always worth it.

We have a few pickups on route to the boat in Larne, as we travel with a few great friends from the Shankhill, Newtownards, and the surrounding areas, as well as more local to where I live. Every trip we sit at the same seating area on the boat and enjoy the banter throughout the day with one another. The crew on the boats know us well with us having travelled over for years and they also give us a bit of craic about the Gers.

After the match when we are heading down towards the boat for home, most times, we have a half an hour to stop in Girvan for fish and chips and maybe even an ice cream.

On a few occasions we have faced problems of ferries being cancelled or delayed. Last season, on an Old Firm day, on our way over, well it wasn't totally cancelled that particular day, but the boat was delayed going over that particular morning. We could see the boat out at sea, it was close to docking in, in prep for boarding. At that time were a bit unsure for a while whether the boat would sail that morning, so we were starting to doubt that we would get to the game. However, eventually we did get to the game, but we just missed Ryan Jack scoring the only goal on that day to win the game!

Also due to reasonably bad weather on occasions, the boats have been cancelled. I can remember one morning we were literally ready to head out the door of the house and phones started ringing to say that the boat was cancelled due to very high winds.

I have had the privilege of getting to many semi finals and finals over the years and have many great memories from all of those games. I have seen Rangers win and lose, and have seen the good, the bad and the ugly, as regards to things that have happened during those games and our rollercoaster recent history.

I had the honour of being one of the lucky Rangers fans to have made the trip over to Manchester for the UEFA Cup Final back in 2008, when Rangers took on Zenit St. Petersburg. Sadly, the game didn't end the way we had dreamed it would, but just being there was a special moment, alongside my Dad. The atmosphere was truly amazing and to see the stadium decorated the way it was with the colour, is something I will always remember.

I have many stories of my times being over at games, such as meeting players, ex players, managers etc. I have had the absolute privilege of meeting the likes of the following:

Walter Smith, Alex McLeish, Marvin Andrews, Sandy Jardine, Willie Johnston, Colin Stein, Mark Hateley, Ally Dawson, Richard Gough, Ian Durrant, Paul 'Gazza' Gascoigne and the list goes on...

I have also had the pleasure of meeting Rangers TV's Tom Miller, on many occasions who has over the time became a fantastic and trusted friend. This has been through times that Tom has been over for end of season functions, here in Northern Ireland.

Some of the above names also have become good friends.

I have also had the honour of getting to know Ally Dawson, Derek Parlane and club historian, David Mason in recent years, who again have become good pals.

I had the honour, alongside my Dad, to be a flag bearer for the day when we were in Division 3 of Scottish football, that was during a league cup game against Falkirk. On that particular day I had the pleasure of speaking to Kenny McDowell, who at that time was assistant manager to Ally McCoist, and I also spoke to Jim Stewart who was goal keeping coach at the time. After meeting Jim Stewart, Jim seemingly watched out a little for me and got to recognise me about the stadium on match days and at Hampden Park, just before kick-off on a cup final day, he came walking over to me and handed me his match day programme.

I also had the pleasure of meeting the genius that is Paul 'Gazza' Gascoigne and on the day that I met Gazza he slipped his training top off and handed it to me. As this was happening, Gazza called the photographers over to take a photo or two, which a fortnight later appeared in the match day programme.

I had the privilege of meeting the late great Sandy Jardine, Mark Hateley and Willie Johnston when they were here in Northern Ireland for a family fun day. At that time my Dad had the honour of being their taxi driver and drove the legends to wherever they wished to go. Dad being Dad, as he always does, starts talking about me and my love for the famous Glasgow Rangers. The 3 legends then decided they would pop up to my school to say 'hullo hullo.' The late Sandy Jardine walked straight in my direction and shook my hand saying 'Hi Timothy, how's things with you pal?' I'm not going to lie, my jaw dropped at that moment.

Later, after school, I arrived home to a massive blue bag sitting in the living room. As anyone would expect, I was intrigued and had to find out what was in this big blue bag. So, I opened it up to find the Broxi suit! Yes, indeed, thee Broxi suit. As any kid would, I just had to try at least the head of Broxi on, even if it was just so that I could say that I actually wore part of the Broxi suit.

Thank you for asking me to contribute, it's been a pleasure and privilege

@timgers12

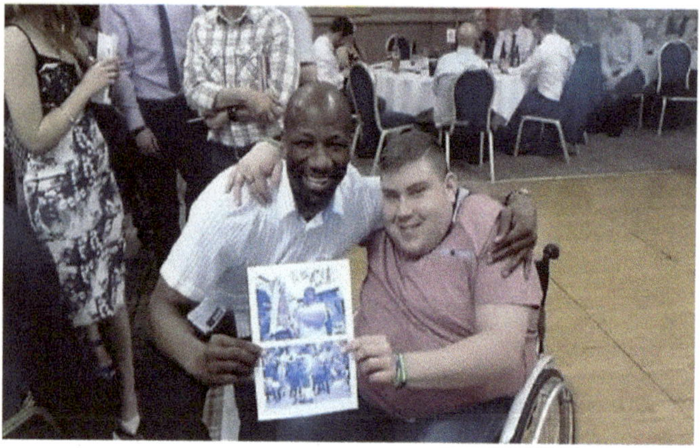

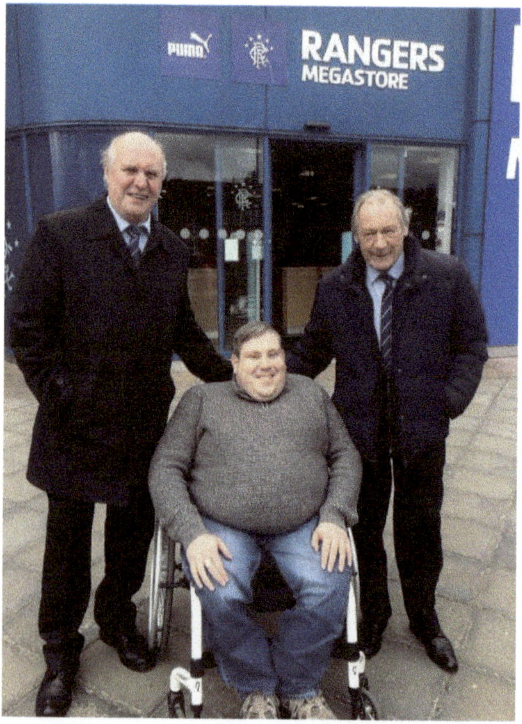
PUMA
RANGERS
MEGASTORE

22: Groningen Loyal on Tour

RB Leipzig 4 v Rangers 0, 15 January 2017
Red Bull Arena Leipzig

Story by: Matt Schreurs Groningen, Holland

As soon we found out this game was scheduled, we started arranging our trip by car from Groningen. It was just 500km to Leipzig, roughly a 4.5-hour drive. I contacted our mates from the Polmont Loyal about tickets and meeting up on matchday. This would be the first European away game for the Groningen Loyal, not knowing what kind of test it would be to get there, but we were very excited.

The weekend of the game had come, 4 of us would drive up on Saturday morning and 2 on Sunday and returning on Monday, that's when the unexpected started. Our driver and owner of the car cancelled just a couple of hours before departure because he had been sick all week, nice timing mate! So instead of 4 of us, it was suddenly 3 of us and no car! After a stressful hour, we arranged a car with winter tyres, for our dodgy winter weather. What could go possibly go wrong now... a lot more! One of us had to come from one of the Dutch Isles and missed his boat which meant a delay of a couple of hours. As you can imagine, this wasn't the way we wanted to start this away weekend to watch the mighty Rangers. When we drove off we all laughed about it and asked each other what else can go wrong........wait for it.

When leaving Groningen up north, you first drive east towards Bremen and then you go down south towards Hannover – nothing wrong until we were just past Hannover, nearly halfway on our trip. Snow, rain, freezing rain and wind nearly made it impossible to drive any further, but we had to, our Rangers family and good German beer were waiting for us. Everywhere en route there were stranded cars and lorries, but one car kept on going. We had to because they started closing highways and roads, but lucky but for us it was roads we had just passed. After a 9-hour drive (double the expected time) we arrived knackered at our hotel and considered going straight to bed, but how could we!

We went straight to the Kildare City pub and had a great night. Joking, laughing and telling others about our trip and meeting our Rangers family from all over Scotland, Ulster and England. After a couple of hours, I was even allowed behind the bar to arrange all kind of Rangers songs.

On matchday we went in RB Leipzig pub first, it's always my mission on an awayday. It was just round the corner from our hotel and we had to wait for the other 2. When we were all together, we went back to the Kildare City pub again, where the Polmont Loyal were enjoying the German hospitality. We put our flags up and let the fun begin all over again. I'm still looking for someone who has a picture of both of our flags hanging in the alley behind the pub – if anyone can help, contact me please. We didn't do the organised walk with the Union Bears, but went to the ground the later, a bit more beer time and it was freezing. Halfway to the ground I had a huge problem, I had to shit and when I have to shit, I have to shit. It was minus 15 and I started sweating and getting worried, that's when I found a snack kiosk and at the back let it all go, watched by a couple of drunk Rangers fans who couldn't believe what was going on 🤭😂

I'm not remembering much from the game, but it was stone cold. The stadium from outside looked really like an old Eastern German stadium, but from inside it looked brand new. And what a sight! 7000+ Rangers in the middle of winter, miles away from home and all those flags. Rangers gave it their all, but at that point Leipzig were 2nd in Bundesliga, so way too good for us at that stage.

What I remember as well was a load of Germans from other clubs in our end who hated Leipzig big time, every single

German loved us, from the old bill, local citizens, taxi drivers and their fans.

After the game, back to the pub of course, for our next sash bash and the pub ended up with no beer anymore.....just some bitter dark German lager left, which we had to drink of course. When I went on a stroll through the pub I found a small bar on the 2nd or 3rd floor with some real lager left. It took the rest more than 1 hour to find out I got my pint upstairs, what a laugh.

So, a journey that started a bit rough with a trip to hell travel wise ended up as one of my best away days in Europe. Looking forward to lots more hopefully.

@tjeu1973

23: No Progrès for Pedro

Fc Progrès Niederkorn 2 v Rangers 0, 4th July 2017
Europa League Qualifying round 1st round 2nd leg

Story by : Linda Smith (Louby) – Fife

Mark and I left Fife on 3rd July 2017 for the drive south to Birmingham for our onward flight to Luxembourg for the game against FC Progrès Niederkorn. A few scary moments on the motorway heading to the airport with some crazy drivers around us. We arrived at the airport with plenty time to spare, so parked the car up then headed through to departures. As we arrived in the departure area there were loads of Bears all over the place…. a sea of red, white and blue.

After sometime shopping and some food, there was an announcement that our FlyMaybe flight was delayed. We eventually took off and the flight was probably three quarter's full of fellow Bears including quite a few familiar faces from travelling around the UK and Europe to follow The Famous Glasgow Rangers.

We landed in Luxembourg airport, which was quite small and headed to the hotel which was a 10-minute walk away. Our son Graham had arrived earlier from London, so had given us directions on how to get there. Once we had unpacked and freshened up, the three of us headed into the city centre to have a look around and to wait for our usual travelling companion Wilf Marshall to arrive from Aberdeen.

Visit to the Stade Josy Barthel – Matchday 4th July 2017
After breakfast we headed to pick up our match tickets. The city centre was bustling with Bears, lots of singing and drinking as is the norm on a Euro away trip. Once we had

collected our tickets, we decided to make our way to the stadium so we knew exactly how to get there and how long it would take us for the game later in the day.

The stadium was only a short bus ride from the City centre and as we walked round the stadium footprint, we found a gate that was open where the TV crew were going in and out to set up their equipment. We decided we would take a wee look in and found there was a running track around the pitch so our Wilf decided he would run a lap around the pitch! The stadium itself was very dated. There were wooden seats at the front of the main stand which had been added to ensure that the stadium met the UEFA minimum seating requirements. We took some photos in the Rangers dugout before heading back to the city centre where we spent a few hours walking around the city.

Off to the match we go…

We decided to go to the stadium early so we wouldn't have to queue to get in. We decided to stand near the back so that we could see over the fence. I don't like having to watch games through a wire fence! However, given the way Rangers played it may have been a more interesting watch through the fence. We were abysmal, the excitement in the first half consisted of a Kenny Miller shot getting blocked. The second half was not much better, Niko Kranjcar hitting the crossbar was the closest we came to scoring. Progrès then scored twice, so that was the end of our very short European adventure under Pedro Caixinha. We sat in shock after the final whistle for about 10-15 minutes and as we were heading out of the ground, one of the refreshment kiosk guys apologised for his team beating us.

As you can imagine every single Bear leaving the ground was feeling exactly the same, shocked and bewildered as to what we had witnessed. We decided to wait to see what sort of reception the team would get from the fans that were still around the stadium. The Rangers team remained inside the stadium for quite a while, probably hoping that the crowd would disperse. Unfortunately, that didn't happen and if anything, it made a lot of fans more annoyed. Pedro made a short appearance behind a fence which didn't help in any way. Eventually the Progrès players began boarding their bus and the Rangers fans still around started applauding them and wishing them good luck in the next round.

When the Rangers team started boarding the coach in little groups, the frustrated Bears made it very clear how disappointed they were with the result.

We walked back into the city centre then got a bus back to the hotel. Wilf decided he needed to go for a walk to calm down and returned a while later with some snacks that he had picked up from a nearby petrol station. We headed to bed to try to get some sleep and had decided that we would still go ahead with the pre-arranged visit to Progrès's stadium the next morning, otherwise it may have looked like sour grapes if we did not go and I certainly didn't want to seem ungrateful.

Whilst staying in a Glasgow hotel the week before for the first leg at Ibrox, I had got chatting to the Progrès Kitman Nobert and some other Progrès staff. Nobert asked me if I was going out for the game in Luxembourg. When I said yes, he kindly gave me his mobile number and said if I needed anything or had any issues when in Luxembourg to give him a call. I had text him before we left for Luxembourg to see if it would be possible to get a look around their stadium during our visit. Arrangements were made for us to be collected from our hotel on the Friday and he would drive us down to the stadium after he dropped the UEFA officials at the airport at 9am.

Graham, Wilf and I headed off with a very happy but very tired kitman. It was about an hour's drive to the Stade Jos Haupert and on the journey there he told us they had been partying and celebrating at the ground until 5am... As we were parking up, all we could see was loads of empty beer bottles, champagne bottles, and glasses from where they had partied!

We got out of the car and were shocked with what we were seeing – there was one stand with a couple of hundred seats and a bendy bus in the corner which turned out to be their hospitality suite! There was a player's lounge on the corner of the stand which was not very big – no surprise that there were more empty bottles on the tables in there! The dressing rooms were in a separate building behind the stand. To access the dressing rooms, we had to walk through the laundry room where there were team strips hanging on coat hangers. It turned out the team didn't have one dressing room big enough for them all, so had to get changed in two separate dressing rooms! We continued looking around other parts of the ground before returning to the car for Nobert to drop us off at the train station for our journey back to the city to meet up with Mark, who had decided not to join us on the stadium visit. This visit just confirmed how bad the previous night's result had been and rubbed even more salt in the wounds, however everyone that we met during the visit were lovely and very accommodating. As we were driving away from the stadium, our host pointed to a building across the road and informed us that was the Post Office where the Progrès Manager worked. When we got out the car at the train station, thanking Nobert for his hospitality, he went into his car boot and gave Graham a presentation gift with a Progrès scarf tied round it. His generosity and friendliness were amazing.

We grabbed a bite to eat before heading to the airport for our flights back to the UK. Apart from the football it had been another good trip abroad meeting up with fellow Bears from all over the world.

I chose to share this story to show how far we have progressed in the last 4 years, both in the League and in European competitions and is one trip that I will never forget for several reasons.

I have been a Rangers fan all my life (now in my fifties) and have great memories from being able to follow Rangers, travelling all over the UK and Europe to watch my beloved team. I have lots of special memories from over the years, especially from the 9-in-a-Row era. I have been lucky being able to watch the likes of Derek Parlane, John MacDonald, Davie Cooper, Ally McCoist, David Robertson, Paul

Gascoigne, Brian Laudrup and Jörg Albertz and feel honoured to have met many Rangers Legends (Players and Fans) over the years who are my Rangers Family. WATP

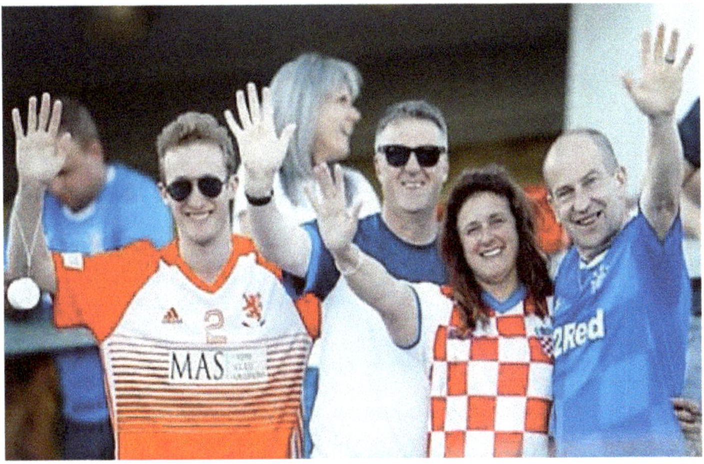
MAS
2Red

24: 'You're going where to watch Rangers'?
FC UFA 1-1 Rangers (AGG 1-2) 30th August 2018
Europa League Play Off second leg
Story by : Brian Taylor – Glaswegian Loyal RSC

I will try my best to keep this short, sweet and straight to the point, but think the build up to UFA alone has its own right to be told. My work decided to relocate premises and gave all employees the information for the new office which is located near Glasgow airport. I thought that it would be fantastic if I could arrange a flight out via Glasgow airport. After a bit of searching on Sky Scanner, I found the perfect flights. However, I still required annual leave during the period of relocation, which I figured would be asking too much, as I had already visited Macedonia, Croatia and Slovenia in previous rounds, so once I found suitable flight times from Glasgow to UFA (via here there and everywhere, about £450 for Heathrow to UFA and £250 for a return Glasgow to Heathrow deal), well suitable flights in my eyes only, as you will find out later on!

The first bump came when a Visa was required, not only did I find myself up at 5am to get the first train to Hibernian territory, I was also already £35 down for the return trip alone. That was the cheapest part of the journey as I was soon to find out. I filled out the Russian Visa with its many sections and pages about my personal information, my close family and then the price of the Visa was confirmed, I was in a rush to receive it in time for my flight. The best part of £160 to my knowledge was the cost, so my passport was handed over and I was ready for my next Rangers adventure.

I managed to sort two days annual leave, as the first departure of the trip was Wednesday night at 6pm. No way was I missing UFA away due to my office relocating, it would be a crime against humanity in my world to not be able to witness Rangers on the brink of getting into the European group stages since 2011. It was simply unthinkable and so was my route to get there and back!

Off I bounce to the airport in such an excited mood about the adventure ahead with only my phone, phone charger, passport, glasses, and Russian money. I did not pack a change of clothes, as I did not class any part of my journey as an overnight stay, such was my determination to get to my destination and hopefully witness history. Glasgow to Heathrow was straightforward, I arrived about 7.30pm and checked in for my overnight flight to Moscow.

Upon boarding the British Airways aircraft to Moscow, it was pretty deserted, which I thought was ideal given that I prefer to pass out on the flights over to all my destinations in the world. So, I settled down and landed in Moscow around 3am their time and got through customs with little problem. However, I had about 10 hours to kill in Moscow, so I found a quiet area and got back to sleep, hoping by the time I wake up I have little time left to kill. How wrong was I come 7am! Airports can be pretty boring especially when you are on your own and hardly anyone speaks English (not that I can be the best English speaker either especially with a few beers in me!), but I persisted with my current location and thankfully come midday my flight to UFA was in sight. God must have been watching over me, as the entire trip was going according to plan.

Moscow to UFA only took about two hours, but different time zones meant I was landing in UFA at 4pm their time. I understand asking Russians in English about transport would not be easy, so I decided to translate a few requests into Russian on a bit of paper, so I could get to the ground. I was advised by a Rangers supporter from Russia to book a taxi at the airport and not jump into the first one I saw, so I took his advice. Taxi booked and on I went to the stadium. The journey only took the best part of 15 minutes and once I arrived, I bumped into a few German Rangers supporters who had also made the trip. I was over the moon I had caught up with fellow fans but had to find the away section now, which was my next task. I asked one of the local coppers who was directing traffic at the stadium about the location of the away end, he then phoned his sergeant for verification and I was then given the phone to communicate with the acting sergeant. There was me thinking it was a sir but I was quickly informed it was madam, oops schoolboy error! After a few minutes we were on the way around the stadium to our entrance, with still 2 hours to kill before kick-off. One of the German bears decided to go find a pub or shop that would sell us some beers.

We found one on the main street next to the ground. The locals looked at us as if we were alien like lifeforms as this was the first time, I was told, any British football supporter had visited UFA. The labels we had on certainly sparked up a conversation, the Russians were wearing Fila and 80's clothing and with me having a Fila long sleeve on they were certainly impressed. I'm unsure if my peers back home would complement me on being behind on the times, but such is life.

Now onto the game. The away entrance was basic and nothing special and the stewards seemed okay with us putting up the Rangers Loyal banners of various supporter's clubs in the stadium and the match begun. Looking around, I must have counted around 40 bears, but some might say otherwise. Rangers made the perfect start when we got a goal through Ejaria and as the game wore on we were in pole position for qualification until UFA made it 1-1 and we then went down to 10 men when Morelos, our lovable hothead, received his marching orders for a second yellow. With about 25 minutes left we were down to 9 men when Jon Flanagan was given a second yellow for a dubious elbow while jumping for a header. This could have been disastrous for us but fortunately, we held on thanks to a string of brilliant McGregor saves. Once the final whistle went there was unbelievable jubilation amongst the tiny band of Rangers fans, Derry's walls could have been heard in China, we were that loud and happy. One of the bus organisers offered me a lift back to his hotel for beer and food before my taxi ride to the airport and for that I am very grateful, cheers Stevie!

4.30am Friday morning and off I go back to UFA airport, the place was quiet and only a few on the routine flight to Moscow. Job done for the first phase and 2 hours in Moscow before another internal flight to St Petersburg. Once I arrived in St Petersburg, I managed to get Wi-Fi in the Irish themed bar in the airport, only to find out through my friend John M back home that I was heading back to Moscow for the group stages. My head hit the table in despair at the thought of doing the Visa again, never mind the travelling. Just as well I had a few beers to calm my nerves!

St Petersburg to Heathrow – by this point the journey had lost its appeal for me, I just wanted to get back and get into my own bed, but one more leg was still due and I had to plan my return to Greenock from Glasgow airport. I then broke the moral code and calmy asked one of my ex's to come pick me up at the airport and take me home, there is a good soul in there somewhere, as she agreed.

Heathrow to Glasgow was the final part of my trip and once I got back the buzz of my journey came returned, as I knew that was it over until the group stages, where I would need to plan another European adventure. Until then it was home to bed with the biggest smile on my face knowing I got to see us make history in UFA.

We are the people.

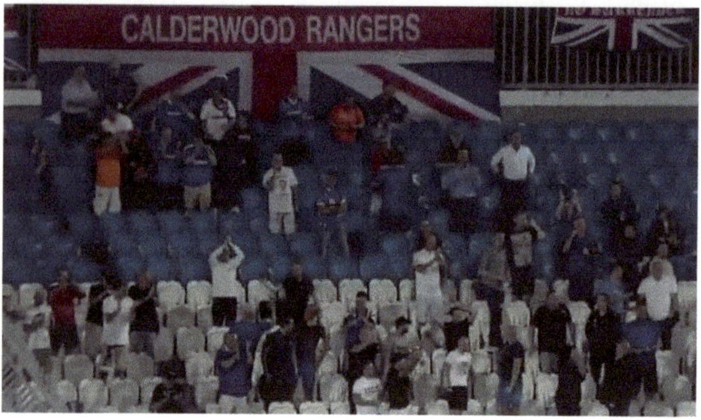
CALDERWOOD RANGERS

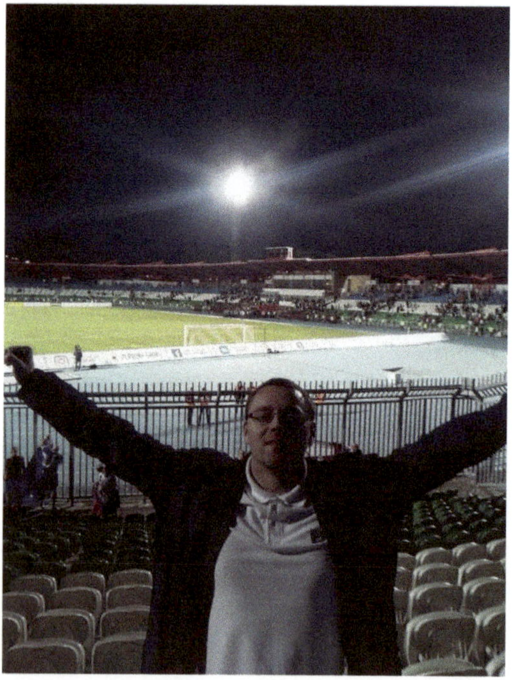

25: Glasgow-Vienna-Benidorm-Glasgow
Rapid Vienna 1 – Rangers 0, 12.12.2018
EUROPA LEAGUE
Story by: Kenny McCallion – Glasgow

Me and my good friend Craig Paton arrived in Austria the night before the game, we found a good boozer and sorted our hotel later. Our first night was great, we drank with the locals, sampled the local food, got to our hotel, which turned out to be a hostel and shared a dormitory with a man from Brazil, the bed was as hard as the streets of Glasgow. On the night of the game we went to bar Bruw for a few beers, well more than a few! We had our match tickets so headed to the game, stopping at a local bar just outside the ground. We mixed well with the Rapid fans and we were in the bar for around an hour or so. I had my bag with my flag in it, then all of a sudden some Rangers fans in the bar shouted and pointed at the door "mate he's got your bag"...but it was gone, I didn't see who took it , some Rangers fans said it was their ultras that had nicked my flag. I'd had the flag for 20 years, given to me by Plymouth True Blues and had added 'Kenny on tour' on the flag .

There it was, flag gone, but worse was to come when I checked for my phone which had my match ticket in the phone cover, it was gone, now the trip was turning into a nightmare. No phone, no ticket, oh and no bank card, as it was also in my phone cover. At this point my mate and I decided I should just make my way to the ground and try and sneak in. We got to the ground, the police were everywhere, turnstiles packed with stewards. I tried but got turned away. I was now feeling sick. I'd travelled all the way to Austria with a match ticket, now everything had gone, even my bank card.

I told my mate to go into the ground. I reported my stuff stolen to the police, but they weren't interested in helping me. I spent all match in the police station reporting my bank card and phone missing, that was a waste of time! The game finished, I stood at the away end looking for my mate as the Bears piled out disgruntled as we had just lost 1-0 in a tight game and were out of Europe.

Remember I have no phone and think I had about €120 on me cash but couldn't see my mate. Instead, I bumped into a few guys I know from the Bristol Bar in Glasgow. So, we headed to the town centre, had a few beers, then for some reason jumped into another taxi and asked him to take me to the nearest hotel. For the life of me I could not remember the name of my hostel. Anyway, I got out at a hotel, went to the bar and bumped into my next-door neighbour, who I never knew was going on this trip. It was surreal and funny at the same time. I also bumped into Agnes from the St Andrews supporters club in this hotel. We had a good few drinks, then I went through my pockets and found a receipt with the name of my hostel, so again another taxi back to my hostel. Of course, my mate was not there when I went back instead he bounced in about 5am, much to the dismay of our Brazilian roommate!

Next day was our last full day, so we spent the time in a few bars and clubs as you do. We were meant to go home early the next day, our flight was at 6am, but we did not set our alarm and I woke up at 6:30am, bawling and shouting as we'd missed our flight! This was now turning into a nightmare trip. The only flights we could get back home were via Alicante with an overnight stay, the connecting flight to Glasgow, at 1pm the next day. So we got up and hung around the hostel, went on Facebook and messaged my mate Sie, from Gers TV, who I was with earlier in the trip, told him my situation and about losing my phone etc, to my amazement he said he got a message from a woman who found it , bank card and €80 plus £30 still in it... No match ticket though, someone had taken that, but she saw my screen saver and knew me and Sie were friends. Anyway, we sat for a few beers after that and a pizza delivery guy was delivering at the hostel and clocked our Rangers tops, he came over for a chat, then joined us for a few beers, his bag was full of food that he had to deliver but he ended up pissed and those pizzas never got delivered!

He then offered us a lift to the airport which we declined as he was steaming... But we got on the flight to Alicante on time, on a cheap German airline, everyone on board was either Spanish or German. My mate crashed out as soon as we took off. We planned to stay at the airport hotel but halfway through the flight a guy clocked my top, "Alright son did you enjoy Vienna?" "Yes," I said but it turned into a nightmare, lost my ticket, phone and bank card, the lot, missed our flights back to Glasgow, so that is why am on this flight." "Nightmare," he said, "where you staying son?" Told him hotel at airport I think, he then said, "give me 5 mins". He came back and said, "I'm John, I have the Ibrox bar in Benidorm, you are not staying in the airport, you're coming with us." Good job I had kept my Rangers top on or he wouldn't have spoken to me. John took us back to his other bar in Albir, The Orange Tree, and his fantastic wife Wilma put us up in a flat above the bar, fed us in the morning, gave us a few beers, even got his barman to take us to the airport the next day. We offered to transfer money when we got home, his words were, "we look after our own". That day on leaving, I promised him I would return next year with the family and we did. If it wasn't for John and Wilma, we would have struggled to get somewhere to stay and eat – the power of the Rangers family summed up in my wee story.

Ibrox Radio

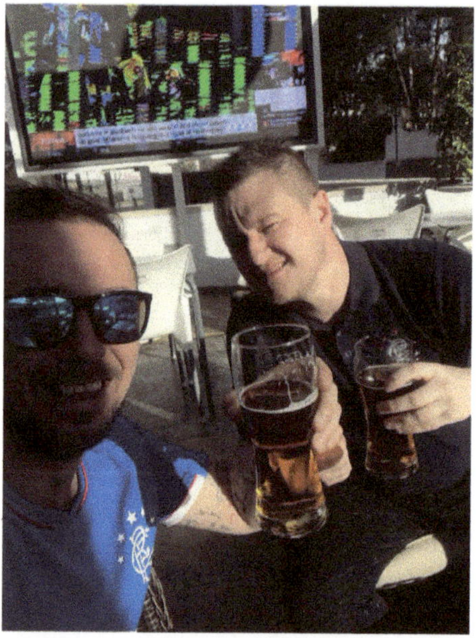

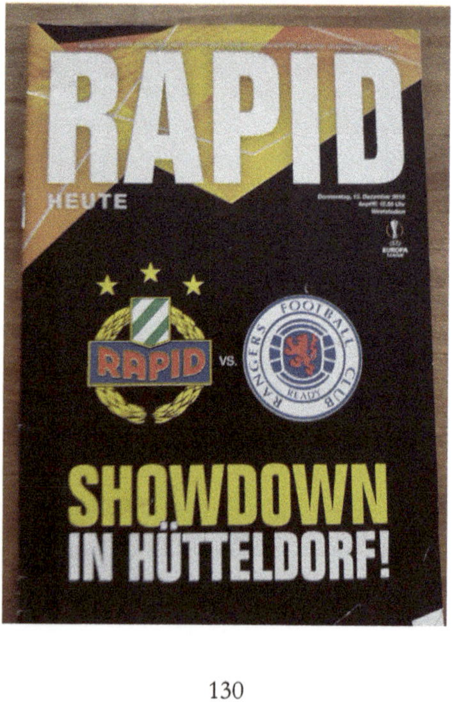
RAPID
HEUTE
RAPID
VS.
SHOWDOWN
IN HÜTTELDORF!

26: Look who is staying in our Gaff!
Feyenoord 2 – Rangers 2, 28th November 2019, EUROPA LEAGUE
Story by : Brandon Stewart – Burnbank Loyal RSC

My story is about my favourite European away match with the famous Glasgow Rangers. I am currently only 22 years of age, so I've only been going to Europe with Rangers the last few years and also home and away in Scotland for the last 17 years. I've been to nine Euro away matches, but the one that sticks out the best for me is Feyenoord away, 28th November 2019. When the group stage draw got made this was the most interesting game out of them all, obviously that mob like to say they're 'friends' with the beggars.

The full build up to the game was a buzz as they hate Rangers and I knew it would be an interesting trip. So around 10 of us flew over on the Sport Options overnighter trip, the flight on the way over was a bit mental and a bit of a blur, as we had a right good drink in us, and we arrived the morning of the match. We had been lucky enough to meet the team on other occasions in the airport and thought nothing of it this time, as the hotel I booked for us was just in the City Centre. As soon as we got to the hotel, I noticed Ryan Kent and thought to myself 'surely not'. We checked in, got the bags in our rooms and went downstairs for a drink. We had hours to kill and there they were – most of the Rangers squad in our hotel, including the Gaffer himself, Steven Gerrard! The team were on decent form at the time, and we really fancied our chances over there, so of course all of us with a drink in us started asking for pictures etc., and even Gerrard came over and had a chat with us asking our thoughts on the game. For him to acknowledge us was absolutely gob smacking, the fact the players and the management team took the time to speak with us and let us get photos, was top class from them. Borna Barišić was rumoured to be injured at the time and him being one of our most important players, we had to ask the question 'is he fit for the game?' Gerrard's words were; "of course he ***** is!" with a big smile on his face. So, after getting photos with the full team, Gerrard and the legend himself, Jimmy Bell, it was instantly one of my favourite moments abroad with the Bears.

My mate had sadly passed away at the beginning of that month and politely asking Rangers security, we gave them a Rangers top with my mate's name on it and it got signed by the full team and I later gave it to my mate's mum, it was absolutely class of them doing that. We cheered the team when leaving the hotel and headed down to the port where my old man and the boys from the bus were drinking and had a sash bash down there before we headed to the game. The set up around the stadium was mental and once we got in the full Rangers end, it was absolutely bouncing and the stadium music gave us a wee song to sing along to – Sweet Caroline!

With wee Alfredo scoring two cracking goals, the celebrations too were madness. Sadly, we drew, scoring 2-2 with them. After the match we felt disappointed not to win, but it was another cracking trip following Rangers with my mates and especially staying in the same hotel as the team and getting that wee 5-to-10-minute chat with the Gaffer, it was one I will never forget.

Following Rangers has always been my thing to do, and I will continue to follow them everywhere, which most Bears do. See the thing is, the best part about these trips are the people you meet through following Rangers – you know everyone, as it's always the same faces every trip and the mates I have made through it, will be mates for life. We all go by the meaning "everywhere, anywhere". Every trip is always memorable, but this one just stood out for me as you read above, the team were outstanding with us, getting to have a chat with them might not have been a lot to them, but to us it meant the world.

I could go on and on but will leave it at that. Thanks for asking me to say my part in this book and I am looking forward to reading all the other guy's stories. Mans of the stories I was not even born when they took place. I will follow Rangers over the world for years to come. WE ARE THE PEOPLE!

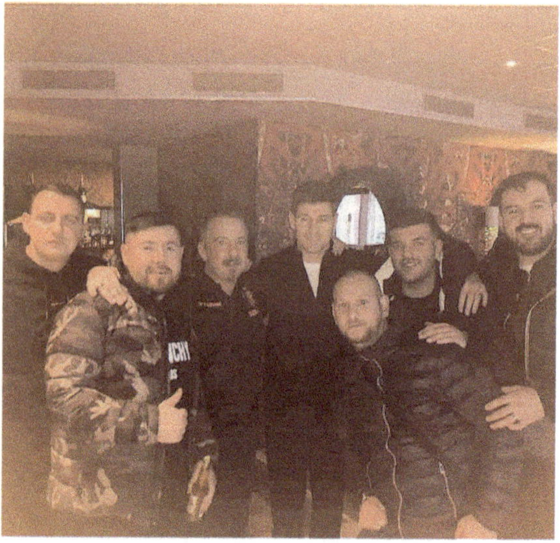

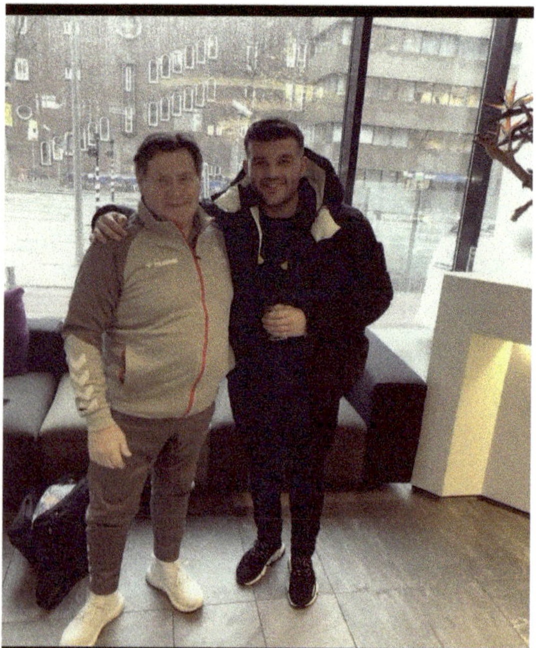

27: Some of our European Jaunts

Story by: John Paterson, Blackpool True Blues,
The Gallant Pioneer
(The best and only Rangers pub in England)

I grew up in Kinning Park not far from Ibrox, with all my family being bluenoses. Rangers were, are and always will be, a massive part of my life. Now living in England, it is even more important to me to make sure Rangers carried on through my two daughters Courtney & Taylor, who were both born in England, but love Rangers nearly as much as their Dad does.

From a young age I was going to games with my Dad at Ibrox and Hampden. In the early to mid-80s, Jock Wallace was Manager and my Granda' and two Uncles, Jimmy & Sammy, had season tickets right on the halfway line in the Govan Front. When I was around 12or 13, this was the 1991/1992 season, and the East Enclosure was bouncing. I remember queuing up at the ticket office for the Rangers v Leeds game from 5am, and then getting to the front of the queue, only to be told there were no Juvenile tickets available for the match and we did not have enough money to buy adult ones. I remember my mate David and I walking away distraught at the thought of missing this game. Little did we know at this point, his Dad was arranging tickets for us, so we got there in the end and WOW that's when I realised what big European nights at Ibrox were all about! Then Rangers were in the first ever Champion's League group stage with Marseille, Club Brugge and CSKA Moscow. That season we went on a 44-game unbeaten run, beating Hibs in the League Cup final with Super Ally coming off the bench to score an overhead kick and then beating Aberdeen in the Scottish Cup final, both games at the piggery to complete the Treble. From then I have had my own season ticket in the Govan front at Ibrox.

At this time, I was getting towards leaving school and I got a placement as a painter & decorator at Glasgow City Council for work experience, to which I thought F*** that, no way am I doing that. So, I wrote a letter to Rangers to ask if could go to Ibrox for my work experience and I got a reply to offer me a 2 week placement on the Ground staff. It was the best two weeks of my 'working' life...... oh and when I left school, I became an apprentice painter & decorator at Glasgow City Council!

In 2002 I ran a bus from Bingham's on Nelson St, where I was working, for Stuart McCall's Testimonial at Bradford. We stayed in Blackpool in the place that would go on to become The Union Bar. The Union was a great Rangers pub and probably just caught the end of Blackpool being a 7 day a week resort, but it was just massive, and sadly closed in 2005. After that our supporters club, Blackpool True Blues, moved to various establishments around Blackpool. I became bus convenor in 2007/2008, just in time for our run to the UEFA Cup final in Manchester. We took 7 double decker's and 2 coaches to Manchester and I'm still bus convener. In 2014 that's when The Gallant Pioneer was thought about purely so we could have somewhere to watch our games. In June 2014, The Gallant Pioneer opened, which I am immensely proud of in conjunction with Jim & Mick. To my knowledge we are the only Rangers pub in England now.

Over the last 7 years we have had great nights with Rangers Legends like Graeme Souness, Jorg Albertz, Arthur Numan, Richard Gough, Ian Durrant, Andy Goram, Mark Walters, Mark Hateley, Lorenzo Amoruso, Davie Weir, Barry Ferguson, Lee McCulloch, Marvin Andrews, Alex Rae, Nacho Novo, Alex Mcleish, Stuart McCall, Michael Mols, Colin Stein, Willie Johnston, Graham Roberts, John Brown, Kris Boyd, Charlie Miller, Scott Nisbet, Derek Johnstone, John McDonald, Marco Negri and not to forget, possibly my proudest moment helping arrange the Legends match at

Fleetwood Town F.C., for our late, great former Captain Fernando Ricksen who was battling MND. That is still Fleetwood Town's record crowd to this day.

When I was around 21, I started travelling abroad travelling on the Nithsdale Loyal buses to Graz, Kaiserslautern, Feyenoord, PSG, Maribor, Victoria Zizkov and there were some crazy times on those buses, before I moved to Blackpool in 2002. By this time cheap flights were now the easiest option, and I've been to places like Auxerre, Porto, Villarreal, Stuttgart, Barcelona and of course, a short trip to Manchester for the UEFA Cup final. Other trips include Vienna, Feyenoord twice, Leipzig, Berlin for a legend's 6 aside tournament, where my now friend Nacho Novo, had a heart attack which was horrible. However, through the years I can honestly say I have never had a bad trip, we've had a few bad results through the years right enough, but there is something special about following Rangers in Europe, which I look forward to passing on through future generations of my family. Perhaps my most memorable trip was Auxerre in the UEFA Cup on 23rd November 2006, during the ill-fated regime of Paul le Guen and the trip was about calamitous, as his reign from start to finish.

There were around 20 Blackpool True Blues myself, Big Mark, Mick J, Billy, Derek, Jim, John M, Tosh, Paul, Alan, Ant, Boothy, Dave, Tot, Mark, Nick, Mick F and Big Wullie (I'm sorry if I have missed anyone out), flying to Charles de Gaulle Airport in Paris from Manchester. We were staying in Paris, when we landed, we've had a few beers en-route. We decide we will jump in taxis to the hotel. It was only 5 euros a head, everyone was fine with that apart from one well-travelled guy Tosh, who hits out with "I know where I'm going, and the train is only 2 euros". We all get in the taxis into Paris, a man down. We arrive at the hotel near the English pub, The Londoner. There are other Bears trying to check in and we hear raised voices at the desk. Whilst in the queue we hear the French guy behind the desk saying to the backpackers, "there is no booking here for you". Then to some fellow Bears, "no booking here for you either". The Bears are getting restless and there are raised voices, as people are not happy with the fact they had already paid for this hotel, only to be told their booking did not exist and he would not refund anyone. It got to our turn in the queue and sure enough, no booking, no refund, so our man in the queue is trying to negotiate showing receipts, booking confirmations, etc., to no avail. The guy was just not interested and kept saying no booking get out. One of the 'older and wiser' members Alan, says let me speak to him and I will try and sort this... within 30 seconds all the Paris tourist attraction leaflets are being thrown across the reception. Then the clocks off the wall, being thrown at the arrogant French receptionist. He's on the phone to the police shouting 'English Hooligans English Hooligans' little be known to us, he had also pressed a panic alarm, and within another 30 seconds the street was surrounded by French riot police with batons out. They had every one of us, except Alan, who had lost the plot and was throwing things, lined up against a wall, as he had managed to sneak out past the riot police as they arrived. Then Tosh who got the train from the airport turns the corner. Much to his amusement we are all lined up against the wall, so he takes his phone out to take a photo of this and a policeman goes mental at him and takes his phone off him. So, we're there being searched and the guy from the hotel is going along the line trying to identify the guilty party (little be known to him Alan was long gone). We are finally allowed to go and the first couple of hotels we try are all full, so we decide to split up and head in different directions. Big Mark and I decide to slip down a street that looks like it has a couple of hotels on it. First one full, second one full, third one, we only have a twin left, that will do lovely, sorted. The hotel had the biggest Alsatian I had ever seen, and it was jumping up us, barking and every time anyone moved in the reception area. No matter what time of day, this dog would go mental and chase you to your room when anyone came in or went out. Think French Fawlty Towers!

We arrange to meet everyone in The Londoner and the place was bouncing. For the first time in my life, I saw someone eat a plate of snails, yes Billy that was you! We all end up in there until closing time, having a great time, songs being sung and bumping into Bears from all over the world.

We then go back to the hotel, only to find the Alsatian is still there under the stairs, so we go in and it goes mental as we walk in, barking chasing us up the tiny staircase to our room, we get in and think what a f***ing day that was, oh well at least it's over and go to sleep.

We wake up early in the morning and my bed is about 2 foot away from the wall and big Mark is there pissing up against the wall next to my head, as you can imagine I'm going nuts ya dirty b****** what the f*** are you doing? He just looks at me and gets back into his bed oblivious to anything he had just done. I'm thinking 'it's match day, it cannot be as eventful as yesterday surely'?

We all meet up in a pub and decide that 3 people will get the train through to Auxerre to secure everyone's tickets for the game and late afternoon, the rest will get the bus from near the Eiffel Tower. We board the bus full of Bears and it doesn't move for easily 20 minutes and when someone asks what the problem is? The whole bus is then told we are not moving until all alcohol is taken off the bus. People then proceed putting all the drink in the hold but some of the Bears think, no chance and hide some on board. Finally, we start to move, only to pull up 200 yards along the road and he refuses to move again, as the bus had cameras upstairs that went straight into the driver's cabin and he had seen someone drinking, so we go through the whole thing again. This happens four times, until there was not a drop left on the bus and we were on our way, 1½ hours late but arrive in Auxerre about 30 minutes before kick-off. We meet our mate who had sensibly got the train and he gave out the tickets for the game and we go into the stadium and the match kicks off.

It's a 2-2 draw, with Nacho Novo & Kris Boyd scoring, but by this time massive questions were being asked of Paul le Guen, due to our terrible form in the league.

On our return bus journey back to Paris. I still don't know where they came from, but a bag of space cakes appeared from somewhere and we had a right good laugh on the way back to Paris!

28: Vancouver to Peterhead without a match ticket!

Peterhead 2, v Rangers 2 – 11th August 2012
Scottish 3rd Division

Story by: Dave Fletcher, Vancouver, Canada

It was Tuesday Aug 7th, and I was driving home from work. I was still upset with what had happened to our famous club. Our first game in Division 3 was only 5 days away, and I knew I had to be there. On my way home from work, I drove to the travel agent to see about a last-minute flight to Glasgow, so I could be there to support my beloved Rangers. The travel agent said there was a flight that left tomorrow morning on a Wednesday but had a 5-hour layover on the way there, in Amsterdam and a 6-hour layover on the way home. I told her to book it. The funniest part was I hadn't told my wife yet or my work, so I booked off work for 5 days and then went home and told my wife that I was leaving the next morning for 5 days to make it to the game. She knows Rangers are my life, so she was happy I was going, as she knew how much I wanted to be there for the game.

There I was the next morning on a flight and on my way, and all I needed now was a ticket to the game at Peterhead. I flew to Amsterdam; it was 9.5 hours to there and then had a 6-hour layover until my connecting flight to Glasgow. Almost 24 hours later I arrived in Glasgow, on the Thursday. From the airport my taxi drove right past Ibrox to my aunt and uncles house, who stay on Copland Road, they were 400 metres away from the stadium. I used to live there when I stayed in Glasgow, from 1998 till 2002. I also used to work at the Rangers warehouse on Broomloan Road.

Friday night, before the game and it's not looking good for me. I was having a hard time getting a ticket, so I wandered down to my local pub, a place I used to work part time at when I lived in Glasgow, the Grapes bar on Paisley Road West. There I was, in the pub and it's getting late, the pints were going down like water, but it was now around 10pm and it looked like there was no ticket for me. At about 10:30pm in walks Tommy Hepburn, who runs the Grapes Bus Loyal and says to me I better get up the road as I have a big game to go in the morning and the bus leaves early. I had tears in my eyes, I was so thankful that he was able to help me get a ticket, and I will never forget that moment. Thank you, Tommy.

There I was at 7am, on my way to the game, on the Grapes Bar Loyal bus. What a bunch of great guys they were, the bus was jumping with excitement for the game ahead. The game, although we drew 2 each, I was blown away by the number of fans that had travelled with no ticket. There were way more fans outside the ground than there were inside. How lucky was I. It was a day I won't forget, as I was there to see my team at our lowest point, and I was there to support them and follow on. I had to leave Glasgow early at 6am so I could be back at work for Wednesday morning, so another 18-hour journey, but it was worth it and I am proud I can say I was there.

In 2015, I flew over for the League Cup semi-final, which we lost to Celtic 2 to 0. I then, was there the next week for the Scottish Cup 2-1 loss to Raith Rovers. It was not the trip I had planned. I was supposed to go home for Valentine's Day, but we were playing Hibs February 13th at Ibrox and I delayed my trip. My wife Ali was not happy, but I told her there were flowers coming to her door and I would make it up to her when I get home.

The game did not go as planned as we lost 2 to 0 to Hibs and it cost me a fortune in changed flights, but I was still there supporting my team win, lose or draw. I keep coming back and would never ever change that, because even though I am in Vancouver, Canada, nothing will stop me from Follow Following the team that I love.

One of the best games I came over for, was with my dad and brother, Jamie Fletcher. My Dad, David Fletcher Sr., was the president of NARSA at the time and he got my brother and I, into the Director's box for the Old Firm game on December 29th, 2018 at Ibrox. What a day that was. When the game started, I could not believe my eyes that Ally McCoist and Walter Smith were sitting directly in front of us. And when Ryan Jack scored, Ally turned around and hugged us!

We won that day, and it was my brothers first Old Firm game ever. As if the day couldn't get any better, we also got to meet Steven Gerrard after the game and got our picture taken with him. That could have been one of the best days of my life and I am so grateful to my dad for arranging it for us.

Although it pains me to not able to be back to celebrate for 55 with all the Bears. Rest assured that Canada Dave will be back, as soon as I can, to Glasgow and to Europe, to support the team I love! WATP.

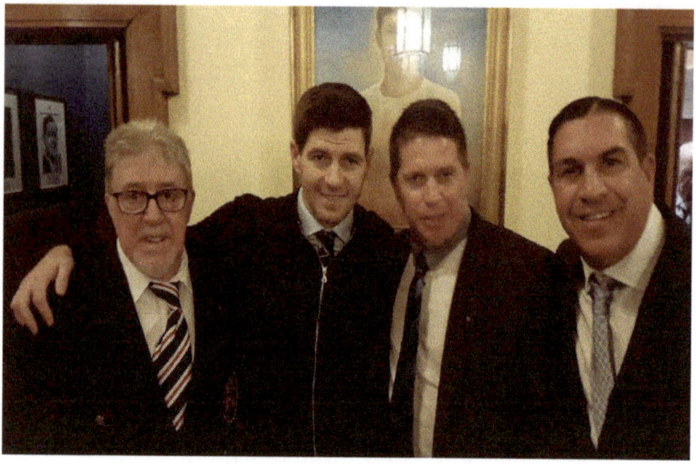

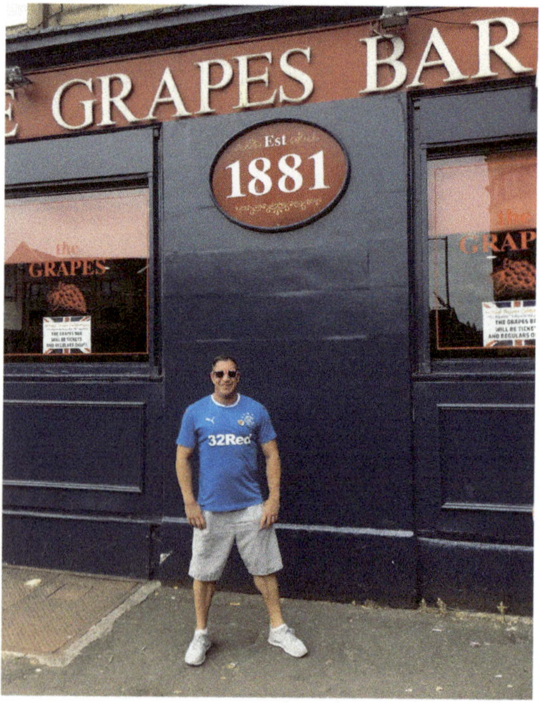
GRAPES BAR
Est
1881
the
GRAPES
32Red

29: The Subbuteo Man

A few Gers stories and memories
George Katsiaris, ATHENS, President of ERSA
(European Rangers Supporters Association)

Born in 1981 in Patras, Greece, I loved and played football ever since I can remember and I was always fascinated by Scotland and the Highlands as well. In the early 90s my father returned from a convention in France, having watched from up close, the UEFA Champions League game Marseille vs Rangers. A few weeks later, he brought me a present for my name day (St. George's Day) a Subbuteo set, which, for the younger ones not familiar with the term, was a popular table football game back in the day. He also bought me an extra team, the Famous Rangers FC. I used to play Subbuteo with my friends all day long back then, so I fell in love with the Gers just from that. I loved the colours, the red, white and blue, and the name, without knowing anything about the team. Love at first sight! Before I knew it, I ended up in front of the TV every Sunday night in order to watch the Scottish Football highlights (it was the only TV football show back then), which were always presented last, while my parents were whining that I need to go to sleep at some point, because I had school the next day. Every Wednesday, I used to walk down to the port (since my hometown has a big port with kiosks selling lots of foreign press and magazines) in order to buy the Scotsman and other Scottish newspapers, so I can read a few more things regarding the team. Those were the times! Nine in-a-row years, the squad was flying and a youngster in Greece cheering for the Glasgow Rangers alone, like crazy, something no one would understand.

Time flies and my first Rangers game finally became a reality. AEK Athens vs Rangers, back in 1994. It's the beginning of August, all Greeks are on vacation, but I forced my father to take me from my Summer house to roasting Athens to watch the Gers (5 hours' drive back in the 90s). Nikos Gkoumas Stadium, AEK's dreadful home ground is pumping but I manage to get a seat (well, no one was sitting down anyway) with the Rangers fans. I had great expectations from that game. A qualifying round and we were to go through to Champions League's last 16, in Group D, along with European Champions Milan, Ajax and Casino Salzburg (nowadays known as Red Bull Salzburg). Brian Laudrup and Basile Boli had signed the previous month from Fiorentina and Marseille respectively, the team looked solid, so I, as well as a lot of people, were sure Rangers would qualify at the end of the day. Unluckily we were to play against one of the best AEK Athens squads ever, with a new addition, striker Dimitris Saravakos scoring against Rangers twice. To be fair, it is devastating to watch your beloved team from up close, for the first time ever, in such a game and end up watching a defeat (I thanked God it was just 2-0). It was mayhem in the ground and in the stands as well. The Stadium was hell, 30,000 people singing through the whole 90 minutes, maybe the Rangers players expected a more relaxed, Summer game? Well, not in Athens! This complacency was something Rangers paid for dearly. In the stands, hell was unleashed as well. I suppose there were no more than 500 Rangers fans in there. We were thrown rocks and flares throughout the whole 90 minutes (plus an hour before and an hour after the game, until we were allowed by the police to leave the ground). I was trying to avoid the rocks and the flares, as well as watch the game and understand what all the other people were singing (a few years later I could speak Scottish all right!). My father and another 4-5 big guys that we just met in the ground were sitting around me, so I didn't get hit by the things AEK fans were throwing at us. Quite an experience! The good thing was that I ended up getting, from the fellow Rangers fans safeguarding me, my first ever Rangers (old school) scarf and a Gers top. I was ecstatic for a week at least, after that, even although we had lost the game. I was hoping the Gers would win the Ibrox tie, but we ended up losing that as well.

In 1996, myself and another 11 friends/Greek Rangers fans, on the Queen's 70th birthday, decide to launch the Hellenic RSC, making it extra special. Watching Rangers from the other side of the continent was difficult back in the day and it was mainly done through newspapers and recorded broadcasts. By the end of 2003-04 season Hellenic RSC was 30 members strong. After talks with the then Rangers Liaison Officer, Jim Hannah, the decision is taken and Hellenic RSC became an official RSC and myself is unanimously elected President. In 2015 Rangers may be in turmoil after the 2012 administration, but in contrast, Hellenic RSC is getting stronger, counting more than 60 members and the decision to form a football team for the members to play looks like more than just a necessity. Sponsors are found, kits are designed and by the start of the 2015-16 season Hellenic RSC Football Team takes shape playing their first friendly game on Monday 07 September 2015. In 2018 it is decided that a football academy is to be founded to educate kids in Greece how to play football with the values, principles and ethos that Rangers embodies.

In 2019, Hellenic RSC being more than 120 members strong, hosts the inaugural European Rangers Supporters Association (ERSA) AGM, in Zante island, organizing lots of events and a charity football match at the island's national stadium (ERSA team winning 3-0). After the ERSA constitution is voted, Hellenic RSC becomes the first RSC to join ERSA as a Tier 1 Member. The first AGM was held, and the board were elected with members from various parts of Europe. Hellenic RSC manages to get 3 RSC members in the ERSA Board while myself, I was immensely proud to be elected ERSA president. In that first convention, we, the Gers fans, set the spark and now everything is in motion! All the bluenoses left the island happy, which was what was needed the most. Honorary guests, Marco Negri, Nacho Novo and Greg Docherty had a great time as well and played with the football team in the charity match. Zante was a success, but the 2020 convention (with Derek Johnstone as club rep, Tom Miller as master of ceremonies and Ian Durrant, Alex Rae and Marvin Andrews as honorary guests) was postponed due to the pandemic. Regardless, a few ERSA members opted to make the trip, so a host of events were organized, as well as a charity match (ERSA team winning 5-0).

The European Rangers Supporters Association (ERSA) are a collection of Rangers Supporters Clubs and fans throughout Europe. The Association was formed to gather Rangers fans around Europe (RSC members or individual ones). The main purpose is to unite all Gers fans under one voice as well as promote Rangers FC, help fellow supporters and fans get together so they can follow Rangers as well as try to increase Rangers' fanbase, around the continent. ERSA promotes social harmony within its own membership and within the Rangers FC global family, always tries to call together Rangers Supporters Clubs as well as individual Rangers fans in the European continent, make them aware of the current formation and ask them to join in. ERSA is of course non-sectarian, non-political and open to all nationalities. Operated on a not-for-profit basis for its members, any income raised is used to promote the Association, as deemed suitable.

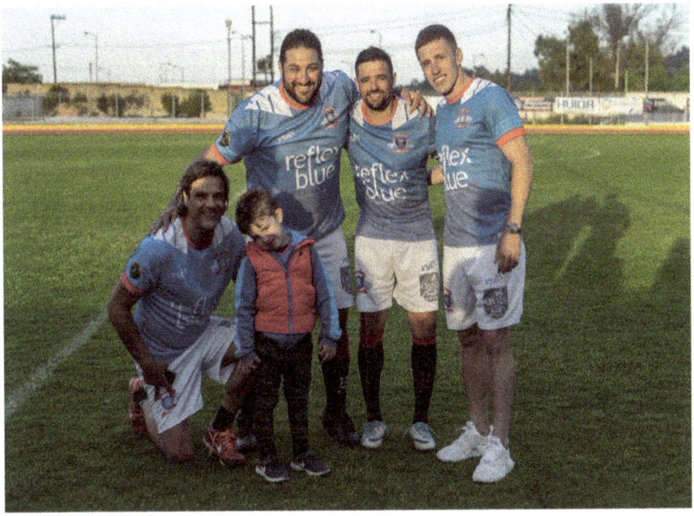
reflex
blue

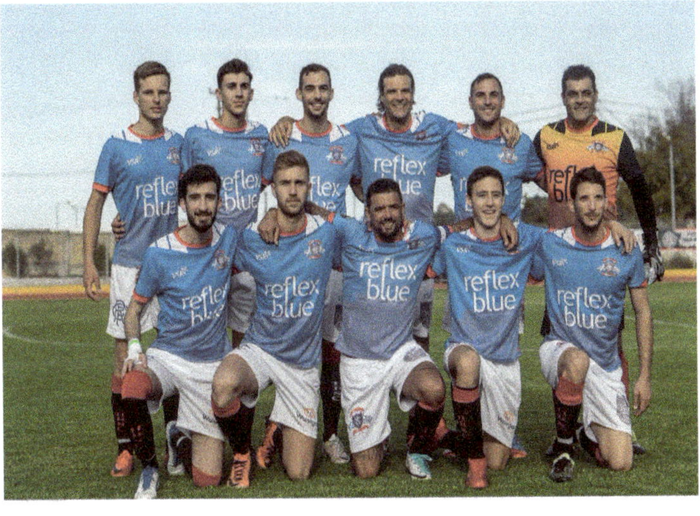
reflex
blue

30: The Union Bears' first invasion of Europe!

Leipzig away January 2017

Story by: Ross McGill – Union Bears (UB) East Kilbride

Late 2016, we began to hear rumours of a possible away fixture against RB Leipzig. I'd go into detail about the history of this club but to be honest, I don't really have anything positive to say about them. They are the complete opposite from Rangers and the values/traditions that we uphold.

Excitement began to build within the support, for many of the younger fans – this was the first European football trip with Rangers, albeit a friendly. As a member of the Union Bears, this was an opportunity for the group to travel abroad together. When more members of our group began to book flights, it was obvious that we were going to have a strong presence at this match. Almost every Rangers supporter I spoke to was also arranging to travel, which made the excitement grow week to week and the countdown to the trip began!

In the build up to the match, we organised a fan's march from Market Square to the stadium, this was our first opportunity to have an organised march in Europe. We were of the opinion from discussions prior, that it would be a short walk and wouldn't take too long. However, on the day we discovered otherwise.

Friday 13th January

Some friends and I from the UB flew from Edinburgh to Hamburg, previously we had decided that we were going to spend the first night in Hamburg and meet up with some friends from there. I'm sure most people know of the club's strong connections to HSV. For anyone who does not, the friendship dates back to the late 1970s when the Hamburg Loyal RSC was formed and since then both sets of supporters have visited each other, and the bond has become stronger over the years; it's almost a guarantee that you'll see Rangers flags & scarves at HSV matches and vice versa.

I'd travelled to Hamburg numerous times beforehand and had spent a lot of time with their Ultras group (Chosen Few) before they disbanded in 2015, so I was looking forward to spending a night in the Reeperbahn prior to a Rangers match. We had a few drinks on the plane, nothing too serious – well on comparison to the night ahead. Once we arrived, we took a taxi to the hotel and literally dumped our cases in the room. Within a few minutes, we were out of the hotel and onto the Reeperbahn, the 24/7 party area of Hamburg. We spent time with friends from Hamburg and other Rangers fans who had travelled there too. We enjoyed a long night in the Tankstelle and the hospitality was superb, as was the familiar song choice which came as a surprise to some of the other Rangers fans who'd never been to Hamburg. A pub in the middle of the Reeperbahn with songs by "The Thornlie Boys" at maximum volume, blaring out of the speakers on repeat, a pleasant surprise for any Rangers fan who hadn't been there before and a confusing one for any Scottish person visiting Hamburg who wasn't aware of the friendship.

Saturday 14th January
After a few hours' sleep and several trips back and forth to the bathroom, I checked my wallet to discover it was now empty. We had arranged to travel to the match with some of our friends from Hamburg who were keen to experience our club & support in Europe. We re-arranged our departure time a few times and eventually plucked up the courage to check-out from the hotel and meet the lads (via a cash machine). The HSV lads had hired a minibus and met us at the Tankstelle, armed with cases of beer and bottles of alcohol, we began our 3–4-hour trip to Berlin.

The tunes again were familiar, probably not too ideal when they are at maximum volume and you feel like you have alcohol poisoning but nothing a few cheeseburgers from McDonalds and some vodka cannot solve. We arrived in Berlin around midday and went to a few pubs before heading to a Beer Hall that hundreds of Rangers fans had taken over. The atmosphere was electric inside, and the songs & chants were in full flow which heavily confused the local band on the stage who continued to play their traditional folk music, frantically attempting to be heard, although they had no chance with hundreds of drunk Rangers fans on tour singing their hearts out.

After a few drinks & some Currywurst – a sausage, curried ketchup and some bread (not my usual choice of food hungover) we headed back to the minibus for our 2-hour drive to Leipzig. It was around evening time when we arrived in Leipzig, once again we instantly dumped our cases in the hotel room and quickly headed out to meet the rest of our friends and the travelling support. As is the case with any European trip, we heard the Rangers support before we saw them and followed the noise to the square. The place was complete carnage, Rangers fans were everywhere, and the pubs were overflowing. It was brilliant, we met up with the rest of the UB lads and other friends who were staying in Leipzig. The HSV lads we travelled with were astonished and said they had never seen a support take over two cities the way we had that day. They were in their element chatting with our fans and really enjoyed the night. These guys had travelled to numerous clubs matches over the years and were all majorly impressed by our supporters.

I did not stay out late because I was still hungover from the night before and I wanted to be up early & be feeling fresh for the fans march along with the game. I said thanks & goodbye to the HSV lads who had come along with us, unfortunately they could not attend the match the next day and had come just to experience our world-renowned support first-hand.

Sunday 15th January
We woke up and headed out to get some breakfast and began our frantic search to find batteries for the megaphone. I had assumed it would be easy enough to buy them, but soon discovered that most shops are closed on a Sunday. Eventually after an hour or so, we managed to find somewhere that sold them and we were set for the march. This may seem like a pointless part of this story but when you're wandering around Germany in freezing cold conditions with snow falling from above looking for a shop that sells batteries then it definitely sticks in your head and isn't easily forgettable.

Off to the main square we headed along with some lads from the group to meet the rest of the UB and everyone else in the Rangers support who had travelled to watch the game. We had some problems with the local Police regarding the march, but we managed to proceed, and thousands of supporters walked to the stadium together in full voice, despite the treacherous weather conditions & heavy snow. The air was full of red, white & blue smoke from pyrotechnics that were set off throughout the journey which looked brilliant. The march did last a lot longer than we had anticipated, mostly due to the local Police but eventually we got there. Freezing, but we had arrived at the stadium.

When we made it into the stadium, we soon realised that our tickets were for a section that was isolated from the rest of the support. This was a disappointment because we'd much rather have been in with everyone else and not stuck in an empty section ourselves, especially since the UB was created to help enhance the atmosphere at matches. However, we made the best of the situation and as a support we produced a loud atmosphere throughout the match. The match itself and result isn't really worth mentioning; the enormous number of supporters who travelled that weekend will always overshadow the performance in that friendly given the circumstances of the previous few years and what the club had been through at that point.

After the match was finished, we headed back to the hotel via buses which had been hired to take everyone back to Leipzig given the horrendous weather conditions. A few of us decided to get a carry out and head to our hotel, a "few" ended up turning into a load of people and before we knew it, a full-scale room party was in motion. It was the final night of a great weekend and eventually we called it a night and flew home the following day.

This game may not have been one of our most important matches or craziest trips, but to me it always sticks in my memory for the younger generation of the support and us as a group. This was our first opportunity to travel in large numbers and organise a fans march in Europe which went really well considering the circumstances and has now became a regular occurrence at every European trip since. The number of Rangers fans who travelled that weekend was phenomenal given it was a friendly in January and the hardship the club had been through in recent years.

Our club and support really is second to none and this experience at the time was a taster for the younger generation of trips to come and a bit of hope for our entire support that natural order would one day be restored, and we'd be back in Europe following our club and at the top of Scottish football once again. Thankfully, we are there and 55 has just happened.

We are back.

@RossMcG1872 @UnionBears_07 unionbears.bigcartel.com

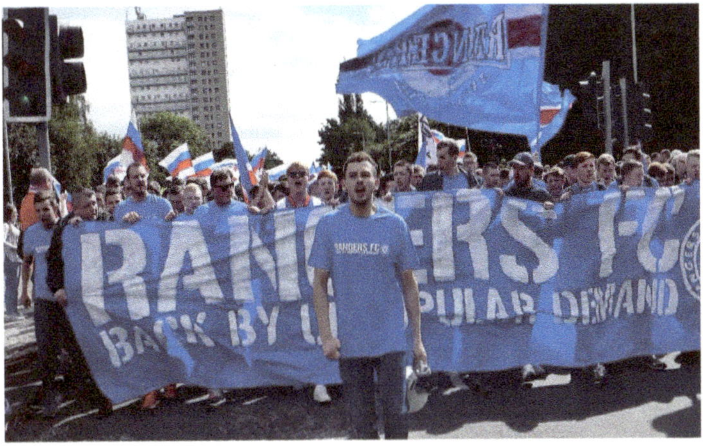
RANGERS FC
RAN ERS FC
BA K BY U PULAR DEMAND

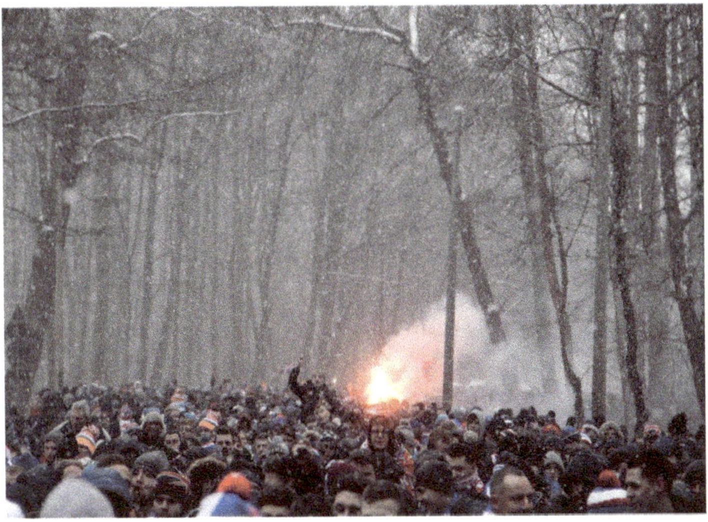

31: Rangers & Romance

The Hamburg Rangers Connection
Story by : Joachim Eybe, Hamburg Loyal RSC

My name is Joachim Eybe, I'm 52 years old, married and father of a fantastic daughter. I was born and brought up in Hamburg in the north of Germany. I have followed HSV all my life and went through all levels of being a football supporter. Started as a young scarfer, got involved with HSVs firm for quite a long time, and worked for a social project helping young football supporters, at HSV and did a lot of work for the official HSV-Supporters-Club which is run by HSV and gave members of HSV a certain influence in club politics and organized away ticketing and offered trips to away matches all over Europe. Nowadays I run a HSV-related clothing- and merchandise shop, with a shop in Hamburg city centre and a few stalls on matchdays around the stadium.

Through two friendly matches between HSV and Rangers in the 70s, there were older HSV fans who were not just members of the oldest HSV-fanclub 'Die Rothosen' (the red trousers, like the nickname for the HSV team), but also members of the 1977 founded 'Hamburg Loyal Rangers Supporters Club'. They were quite active and put pieces about their experiences with Rangers in one of the very few HSV fanzines at that time and were always willing to tell a story, or to bell out a Rangers chant. The Gers were always my Scottish team, but it took some more years before I saw my first Rangers match.

The easiest way to see Rangers live would have been the match v CSKA Moscow that was played in Bochum in 1992. However, I was in the army at that time and was not allowed to leave the base, so I still had to wait. A few years later things had changed a lot. I had left the hooligan business, earned good money, travelling got cheaper and easier and my favourite HSV player of that time, just had signed for Ranger, you know who, Der Hammer. Further on HSV finished 5th that year and played Celtic in the first round of the UEFA Cup. Through already existing contacts with Ranger's supporters, HSV-Fans got made welcome wherever they got to in Glasgow with hundreds of HSV-fans drinking in the Louden Tavern in Duke Street. Hamburg won 2-0 at Parkhead. Through all this I saw the time had come to finally get my arse in gear and go to see Rangers. One of my first Rangers-contacts, a funny guy from Ulster who seemed to go to nearly all Rangers matches home and away, told me about Rangers playing a friendly tournament in Amsterdam. This was the first time I saw Rangers live and some of the guys I met first time at Amsterdam back then, are still going regularly to all matches and it is always a pleasure to meet them. Just a few months later I saw my first Rangers match in Scotland when Rangers played away to Hearts, the last match of the season.

I joined the Hamburg Loyal RSC, in 1996, so I have been a member now for 25 years. We are not a big club, but at the end of the 90s we were quite active and had members of the club at a lot of European away matches. There were also strange situations like 1997 in Gothenburg when eight of us were not allowed into the Rangers end for being German and so we had a whole sector for ourselves. We also went with some HSV & Rangers supporters to matches at Strasbourg, Leverkusen, Eindhoven etc and had buses going from Hamburg to Munich and Dortmund etc, etc. Whenever it was possible to see Rangers in Europe we went and twice we had the pleasure to mix Rangers in Europe with HSV matches in Europe. The night before Rangers played Danish team Herfoelge BK, HSV were playing their CL qualifier v Brondby in Copenhagen. This made it easy for us to see both matches and just a few months later HSV played one night away to Juventus and Rangers the following night in Austria v Sturm

Graz. Also fantastic were our parties for the 30th at the Glaswegian Bar, the 35th in the Wee Rangers Club and in real style at Ibrox for our 40th anniversary.

For quite a while me and my girlfriend at that time and now wife, made no other holidays than going over to Scotland to see Rangers, some years it was 4–5 times a year we went over. It got a bit less when our daughter was born in 2006 and as I always preferred going to away matches, I only went few times after Rangers went into administration, as I knew tickets in all those small grounds were really limited. I still love going to Ibrox but nowadays it is just once or twice a season.

As the Hamburg RSC we have got very good connections to the 'Glaswegian Loyal' who also became a HSV-Supporters-Club and come over to Hamburg quite often. I met their main man Hunter Smith first time nearly 20 years ago when Rangers played Anzhi Makhachkala in a 1-match-decider in Warsaw. I went to Berlin the night before to take first train to Warsaw in the morning. When searching for a seat I heard the familiar sound of the Scottish accent. I joined Hunter and his mate Mitch for that trip and we found out we had common friends. That was a funny trip, especially as I only had a one-way ticket to Warsaw and had to jib the train back. We kept in touch and Hunter has become a good friend of mine.

I also have good contacts to the Queen Street True Blues. Stevie Campbell also was one of the lads I met when going to that Euro 6's Tournament in Amsterdam back in 1997 for my first Rangers experience.

There are so many fantastic regular contacts on my trips, members of different clubs from England, Scotland, and Ulster and it is always a pleasure to meet most of them, it does not matter if they are members of by example the '1st Newry RSC', the 'Union Bears' or the 'Rangers ICF'. It's always good fun.

For me it's difficult to name one best European away trip out of over 50 matches I had been to (including a few friendlies). It was far too many good matches and great fun.

Does not matter if it were Paris in 2001, Stuttgart in 2003, Bratislava in 2005 or Barcelona in 2007, they were all great. I would like to pick out three matches for different reasons that are amongst the Top 5 for me.

2008 – Fiorentina v Rangers (Semi-Final UEFA-Cup): Three of us were flying from Bremen to Milan and hired a car to get to Fiorentina. Through a contact at HSV, we got tickets in the main stand. The Italians sitting next to us were not too happy about us, as they soon found out we were Ranger's supporters, but at least there was no trouble. The view onto the Rangers end that night was fantastic and the moment Nacho Novo's penalty secured being in the final, was magic. It was not that much the whole trip, but the importance and the outcome of the match and the situation when my mate Sven, just after the final penalty went in, got a phone call from a guy he knows, who strangely enough supports not just HSVs local rivals but also that green lot from the east end of Glasgow. He was telling Sven he had two tickets for the final in Manchester. He must have thought Celtic could make it to the final when he ordered the tickets and of course the last team he wanted to see in the final were Rangers. Even that source of two tickets for the final was strange, but we were happy when we left Fiorentina as we knew we would be at the Final. Manchester here we come!

The Final in Manchester was impressive, not that much on the pitch, but to see the numbers of Rangers fans who invaded every part of Manchester. That was a great day, especially as it was my fourth wedding anniversary and my Mrs let me go no problem, as she knows how much I love Rangers. The disappointment of losing the final was quite big even, I never expected to see Rangers in a European final in all my life.

One trip I really enjoyed was last season in the Europa League, when Rangers played away to Porto. I went on the Tuesday and met up with a good friend from Hamburg in the evening near that river, with the big bridge where all the restaurants and bars are. l and met up with some good friends from Glasgow, we had a couple of drinks and a bit of singing the usual songs.

On match day we met a lot of good friends for a pint and a chat and enjoyed the drinks in the sun. The match and the atmosphere in the ground were great and after a few final drinks after the match, this time it was early back to the apartment as my flight left early on Friday morning.

Another great day for me with the Rangers away in Europe was Leverkusen in 1998. We went by car with two friends from Ulster who stayed in Hamburg at that time and my girlfriend. We had a few drinks before the match in Cologne and met a lot of good friends throughout the day. We got back to Leverkusen in the afternoon, the atmosphere was fantastic and in an incredibly happy mood I asked my girlfriend somewhere in Leverkusen, if she could imagine being with me for the rest of her life? As she said yes, we got engaged in one of the worst looking places in Germany. Not very romantic, but a reason to remember that day, not just for Rangers winning that match.

And by the way, my Mrs and I got married a few years later and are still together…

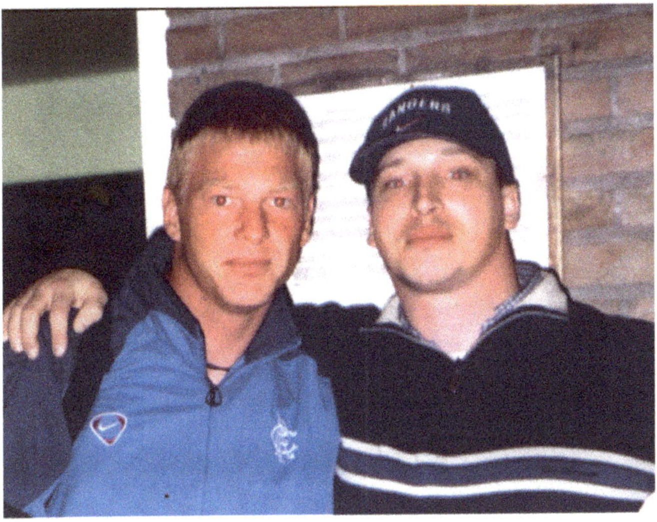

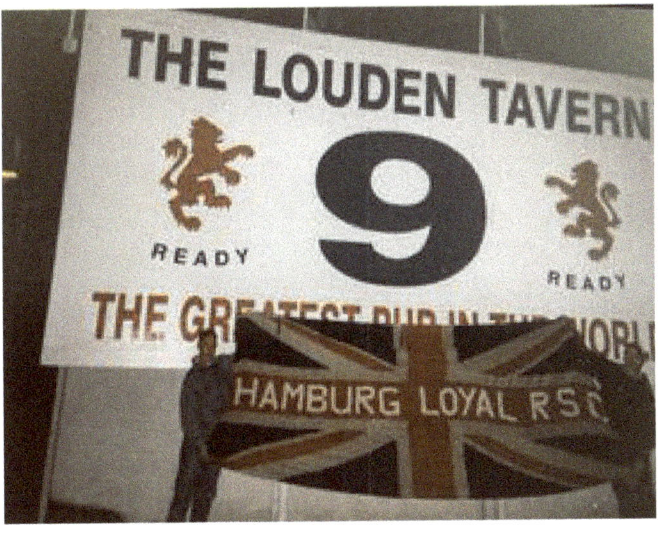
THE LOUDEN TAVERN
READY
9
READY
HAMBURG LOYAL RSC

32: We Best Keep Quiet, Then Bang, Roofe Scores

Standard Liege vs Rangers – 22nd October 2020 Europa League.

Story by: Stevie Campbell and the lads

To the best of my recollection, the Rangers fans in attendance at this match with limited capacity (restricted to 4000 tickets) were: Myself, John MaCaulay, John Galbraith, Callum Benham, Connor McLachlan, Steven 'Harry Potter' Mollins, Ross Blyth, Ralf Kricke, Angelica Heussen, Ross McPherson, Dan from Leicester, Ralf Kricke's mate, Mirko Wozny. In the aftermath of the fixture announcement, Callum contacted a couple of Standard Liege fans he knew called Lenny Janssen & Geoffrey. They managed to do our travelling party a massive favour and supply us all with match tickets, including a couple of complimentary hospitality places for both Callum and I Both guys were a pleasure to deal with, with Lenny shelling out 150-Euros upfront to buy the tickets for us before we squared him up upon receipt of the tickets being emailed across.

Travelling to Belgium

Our group travelling on Thursday 22nd October was myself, John Galbraith & John MaCaulay (and we would meet up with the others across there in Liege). Initially we had booked return flights from Manchester to Dusseldorf on the morning of the match, returning on the Friday morning the day after the match. However due to the ever-changing Covid landscape, these flights were cancelled so we had to rethink our plans. We decided to fly from Glasgow to Brussels via London on the day of the match. We had to do our best to structure the trip to circumvent some of the new restrictions that were put in place – namely having to provide negative Covid tests upon landing and having to isolate upon returning home. At the time, flying into Belgium or Germany directly from Glasgow, would mean legally having to provide negative Covid tests due to a UK-wide hotspot map, that had Glasgow in a red zone for infections – whereas London was a yellow zone and therefore no negative Covid test required. Flying home to Scotland from Germany (at the time) would also ensure for all our group that no self-isolation/quarantine period would be required, either. This was essential for the guys who had work commitments.

Arrival in Belgium/Liege.

Upon arrival in Brussels we were already aware of the state of the play in the country due to Covid and the restrictions that were in place – essentially meaning no bars or restaurants open for us. When we got to the train station me and John collected our train tickets from the self-service machine. We arrived in comfortable time for our train. We boarded on time and set off to Liege. The only thing of note from the train journey, was me getting a couple of warnings off the ticket inspector for constantly forgetting to have my mask on.

We arrived in Liege approximately an hour and a half later.

We phoned some of the other guys upon arrival in Liege (Callum Benham, Connor McLachlan and Steven 'Harry Potter' Mollins) as these guys had booked a cheap hotel room at the 'Univers Hotel' near the train station, due to the fact that the town was on lockdown with nowhere open for us to go.

The guys at the hotel had made alternative travel arrangements to ourselves. After meeting up with the guys in their hotel room, we went a walk and got some food from Burger King and some beers to take to the hotel room to rest up, kill a couple of hours and then plot our next move. Our next move was to get taxis up to another hotel to meet our friends Angelica Heussen and Ralf Kricke from Holland and

Germany, respectively. On route to getting our taxi, we bumped into Ross Blyth, another Rangers fan. Their hotel had the hotel bar open which appeared to be a rarity in Belgium, during their lockdown, sadly only hotel guests could buy alcohol, meaning the rest of us couldn't get a beer and socialise with them. However, all was not lost, as I had contacted Angelica to fill her boot of her car with boxes of beer for us. It was then just a case of blending in with our beers, disguised from the hotel staff and management.

The stadium & match itself

We left the hotel and got some taxis up to the stadium on the outskirts of town. We had to be up at the stadium for a certain time due to myself and Callum having to meet the Belgian Geoffrey, to sort out our hospitality passes for the match. The stadium appeared to me to be in the middle of a big industrial area on the river with lots of units, factories, car parks and not much in the way of anything else (except for some flats and a couple of shops that were closed anyway).

Kick-off and Rangers started in their usual manner – calm, assured, organised. We were playing alright and took the lead maybe slightly against the run of play. I would not say we didn't deserve it though – some folk might say the penalty was soft but to the letter of the law it was a penalty. I thought Standard Liege finished the half the stronger team. The last ten-minutes of the first half I thought we were under the cosh after seeing Standard Liege pepper our goal mouth and hit the bar a couple of times. We were glad to get in at half-time ahead and hopefully kick on fresh in the second half.

Mother Nature had other ideas however.

What followed I've only ever experienced at another Rangers match-Charleston Battery in South Carolina in the summer of 2016 when a lightning storm and flash floods left the match in the balance. It was within 15-minutes of being abandoned before it ever started). The conditions in this match strangely suited us. I know it's the same for both sides, however when holding onto a 1-0 lead away from home when the other team has no choice but to attack, it worked in our favour without doubt.

In a strange way it looked like we embraced these horrendous conditions and used them to our advantage, by letting Standard Liege try and pass it around us in the final third with the ball getting stuck on the pitch and nothing flowing for them as a result.

What happened next – WOW.

Like every other Rangers supporter, I was screaming (inside my head obviously) for Roofe to take it to corner flag and run down the last minute of the clock but what the hell do I know? 55-yards out, he shoots – GOAL.

After the match & returning home.

We were flying home the next morning (Friday 23rd of October) from Dusseldorf Airport, so we had a taxi booked from outside the stadium to take us there on the 3-hour drive. We had booked a people carrier for 6 of us. I won't name the well-known taxi company involved, as they tried to shaft us on the cancelation policy to take us to Berlin Airport from Poznan after another Rangers group stage game (I had to get my credit card company involved to get my money back). Whilst waiting for our driver to arrive, we met up again with Angelica who gave us the rest of the beer from the boot of her car for the journey to Dusseldorf. This was a God-send, as there was nowhere open after the match and it meant we could just get right out Liege delighted with the result (with a few beers to celebrate in the taxi and pass the time).

A nice group of Liege fans speeding off from the stadium decided to drive fast through (what seemed like) the biggest puddle ever, soaking us all head-to-toe, whilst waiting for our taxi, but you know what? We didn't care. Who cares? We were still on a high and running on utter adrenalin.

The taxi ride was fantastic. We got the driver to hook up Connor's phone to his Bluetooth where we had a little Sash-Bash in the back, beers flowing everyone feeling on top of the world after what we'd just witnessed inside the stadium. A quick piss stop/beer top up at a 24-hour service station enroute to Dusseldorf Airport, to kill the last bit of the journey was welcomed by us all, before arriving late on at our Airport Hotel for a late check-in, with our early morning flight home in mind. I think we got about 3 hours' sleep in total, but it was worth it – a trip to remember for numerous reasons.

I'll always feel privileged for being in attendance at this one.

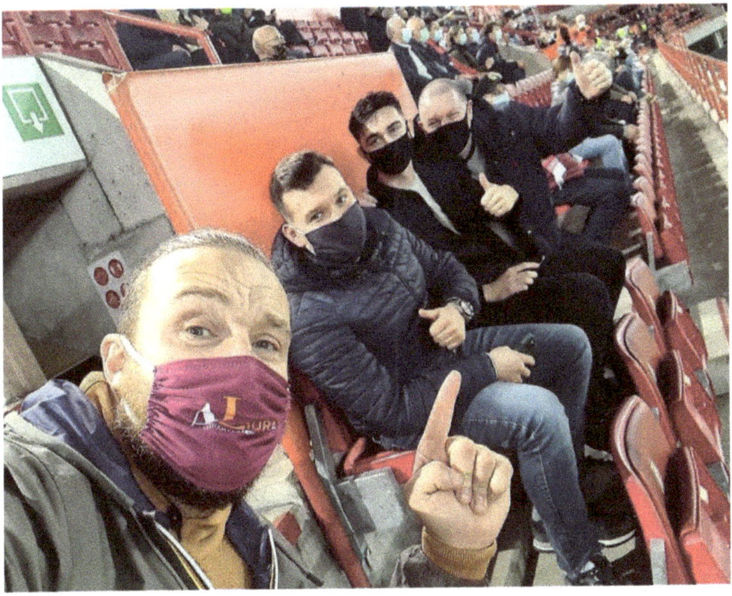

33: We May Be Down Under, But We Still Follow, Follow

Trips back home from Oz to watch the Bears

Story by: John Magee, Rockingham Rangers Supporters Club, Nr Perth, Australia

I was brought up in Hillhouse, Hamilton, living in the schemes with some great Rangers legends including Davie Cooper and Jim (Jazza) Bett, I was lucky to have known them as a boy. I remember Davie Cooper coming around to Jim Wilson's place in Hillhouse, at the flats on Townhill Road after training, we would play heady tennis out the back and Davie would join in. What a pleasure to be with and what a gentleman he was, he is also my all-time favourite Rangers player.

Davie was a member of the Lariat Bar RSC, he was a Rangers man through and through and he would never hide it. Another two great local players to me were Derek and Barry Ferguson. I knew Derek very well, played against him at primary school and then with each other at Earnock High. We ran about together; they were great days. I remember we were in a woodwork class together on a Monday talking away and he got pulled out to go to Malta as Rangers were playing Valletta, he was the youngest player to play in Europe for Rangers I think, the aggregate was 18-0 over the two legs.

I was brought up a staunch Rangers supporter influenced by my Dad, John, who everyone knew as Irish John, he was from Belfast and my mum was from Airdrie. My first game was in 1976, I was 9 years old, it was against Motherwell and big DJ scored the winner, 1-0. We used to go on The Jaffa Bus and drank in the Clansman, Burnbank and what a bus it was!

My favourite cup final as a boy was the 1978 Scottish Cup Final, 2-1 against Aberdeen at Hampden, the year of the treble. We were on the old black double decker Clansman bus, I think it was called the battle axe, with no windows, at old firm games, especially. Every game there was always something happening. I went to that game with my old man and a few of his mates, one being Archie Balfour, who now lives in Benidorm, but we keep in touch and I saw him when I was over in 2018 for the 12th.

My first European game was not the quietest, over in Dublin in 1984 against Bohemians. Kai Wales organised the bus from Burnbank and we teamed up with big Stuart Daniels' buses at the Red Lion Bar, Kinning Park. I had never seen anything like it as we arrived at midday in Dublin. There were only 6 buses to start with and it was bedlam, as the rest of the supporter's buses did not arrive until around 6pm that night, just before kick- off. The rest is history, if you were on that tour you know what I am talking about. It was mayhem!

I left Scotland for Australia in December 1996, with my wife who is Australian. I joined the Rockingham Rangers Supporters Club in 1997. The Club was formed in 1983. We used to get together with the Perth RSC for all the finals. Back then there would be around 400 to 500 of us meet up in Perth, it's now the biggest supporters club in Australia. Our two clubs go from strength to strength. Rockingham is a coastal town one hour south of Perth and we watch the games at the Rockingham Bowling Club. The RRSC is getting bigger all the time. I am now Vice President of the Club and as we speak, we are well over 100 members and have people joining all the time. We have ex Rangers players Ian Ferguson and Gary Stevens always coming to the Club for functions. They are now Honorary members and great people, who love the Rangers!

Another story I'm proud of was when we hired the plane which the two clubs RRSC and the PRSC paid for with the banner '3 in a row Glasgow Rangers Champions'. This was when Celtic were on tour in Australia. They played Perth

Glory that day, and the plane kept flying above the park. Neil Lennon's face was a picture, and our Fergie was the Perth Manager at the time, it was pure gold. Fergie still goes on about it as one of his best days ever, looking at Lennon staring above and shaking his head in disbelief.

Rangers did a tour in Sydney 2010, that was a brilliant tournament. Hopefully, they can come back soon. It was great, a few of us even had a few beers in the pub in the morning with Durranty, as the rest of the team had gone surfing. My mate Rab Crerar is good mates with Durranty, as they are all District Bar boys. Ian Durrant walks into the pub that morning, he has two plastic bags full of training gear and says 'dish them out to the troops'. Shorts, tops, you name it. What a day we had in Sydney with Durranty, great memories were made.

I will finish off with my favourite trip. Coming back home for Manchester 2008, I have never seen anything like it as in supporters wise, unbelievable! Only Rangers could have done that. Walking through Manchester bumping into faces I had not seen in 30 years. It's giving me goosebumps as I remember it now.

We, the RRSC, took about 25 members over and I will tell you this: some of the lads, because of work commitments, basically got off the plane watched the game and went straight back to Oz. That's loyalty!

We based ourselves in Blackpool and were drinking in the Ship Inn. As we were getting photos taken with the RRSC West Australian flag, a news reporter from the BBC Scotland says, 'can you unfurl your flag again so we can film it', which we did, and we were live with Jackie Bird (which I didn't know, I thought it was a wind up). Anyway, the phones started going mad and one of the lads in Burnbank who could not make it, says 'Haw Magee, you only arrived back in the UK 24 hours ago and you are on the TV already!' You couldn't make it up!

As we are fast approaching 55, be assured fellow Bears, we really will be doing the Bouncy all over the world!

GLASGOW RANGERS F.C.
ROCKINGHAM LOYAL R.S.C.
WEST
08

ROCKINGHAM LOYAL

34: A Final Wee Story

John Carmicheal –Snr
Owner of the famous Glaswegian Bar 1994 – 1998

I am honoured to be asked to take part in this Rangers supporters stories book, I must thank Stan and Stuart for letting the Rangers fans tell their stories.

I was born in Dalmarnock, 5 minutes from Bridgeton Cross, a Rangers stronghold. I first started going to games on the Bridgeton Loyal supporter's bus. We ran a football team from our supporter's club and played in the old Rangers News league for supporter's. I was player coach, and we had some great tussles with the other clubs.

In the 90s, I opened the Glaswegian Bar in Glasgow. There was only one choice for me, it was always going to be a Rangers bar. We had visitors from all over the world dropping in before matches, and anyone who remembers our Sunday afternoon session with singer Bobby Parks, it was legendary

Although we have been closed for years now, we still have a supporter's club named after the bar. I also ran the Windsor bar at Bridgeton Cross for a few years, another great wee Rangers pub. One memory is of when we raised £2,000 for the Rangers blind supporters to get them some new audio equipment.

I have been lucky over the years to meet and end up friends through having my Rangers bars and following the Rangers across the world. We are a Rangers family and, in my opinion, the best and most loyal fans in the world. This year we are going to celebrate 55 and it will be an amazing turnaround for our great club. From being kicked to the bottom division, to now topping the league once again, and back to where we belong. It is our time to celebrate. It's coming home…

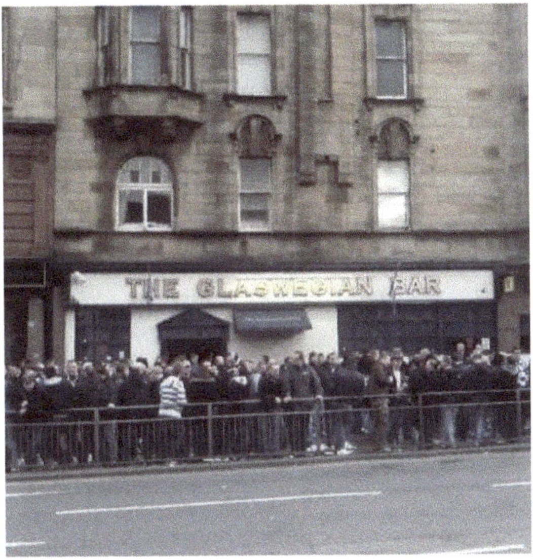
THE GLASWEGIAN BAR

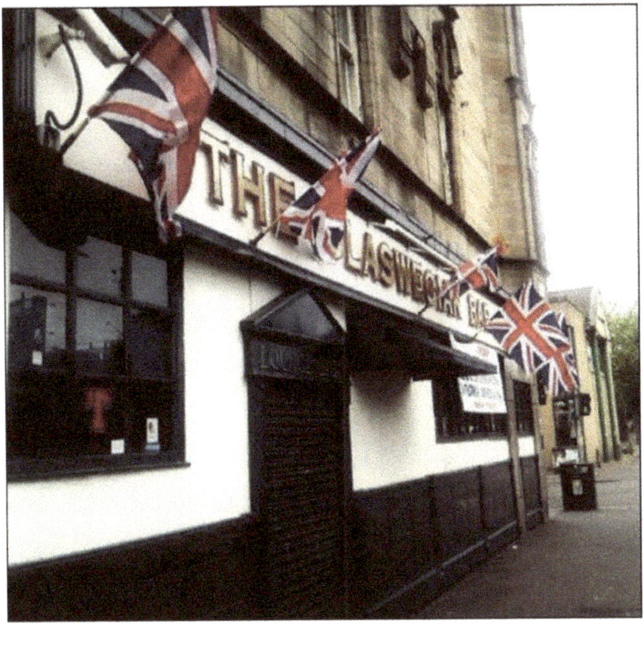

Lightning Source UK Ltd.
Milton Keynes UK
UKHW020223080621
385090UK00007B/361